PRAISE FOR *GROWL*

"*Growl* gives us a front-row seat to the inner workings of the animal rights movement during the past forty years. Stallwood provides a thoughtful review of the theories, strategies, tactics, and—yes—personalities that have propelled the movement's growth and fueled its increasing sophistication.

It's a fascinating story and a good read, as well as an honest, tough, and occasionally provocative analysis of the strengths and, more interestingly, weaknesses of the modern animal rights movement. His discussion of the major currents of thought that have shaped the movement—the spiritual, the ethical, and the political—is concise and insightful, and places animal advocacy squarely within a social justice–movement framework.

Although his Grumpy Vegan persona remains intact and despite the book's title, Stallwood's other side shines through in this book—one that is compassionate (as he precisely defines the term), candid, and self-reflective."

—**Beatrice M. Friedlander**, Director, Animals and Society Institute

"Cruelty to animals is abhorrent to most people and many animal protection organisations have been established. Yet animal exploitation remains commonplace. In examining this paradox, Kim Stallwood's *Growl* considers the value of animal life and offers a unique insight into a lifelong discovery of what that truly means."

—**Chris Williamson**, Labour MP for Derby North

"Not all souls sing; some growl—for justice, for truth, for nonviolence. In this compelling book, Kim Stallwood offers frontline reflections with feet-on-the-ground theory, centered in compassion."

—**Carol J. Adams**, author, *The Sexual Politics of Meat*

D1566593

"If you read just one book this year about animals, make it *Growl* by Kim Stallwood. This stand-out text chronicles Kim's journey from industry insider to a leader in some of the most important advocacy agencies in the world. Without a doubt, Kim is on the front lines of our common struggle to recognize that all life matters, regardless of species."

—**Colleen Patrick-Goudreau**, speaker, educator, and
award-winning author of six books on vegan living

"Combining historical and philosophical thinking with personal experience, Kim Stallwood analyses the origins and growth of his lifetime work advocating for animals. In this engaging and accessible narrative he explores different ways of thinking about—and acting towards—nonhuman animals in order to change the lives of us all."

—**Dr Hilda Kean**, formerly Dean of Ruskin College, Oxford

"On compassion, and our role in social transformation, Stallwood examines our relationship with ourselves, others, and the ability to continue to develop personally. Compassion isn't always comforting; for as much as it is essential to further the animal protection cause, it can be challenging on a personal level, and perceived as confrontational to those we seek to influence and change."

—**Jasmijn De Boo**, Chief Executive Officer, The Vegan Society

"This is a fine introduction to animal rights. A writer with verve and flair and rare honesty, and somebody who was there right from the beginning, Kim Stallwood has stayed fighting the good fight all these years. Reading his book reminded me why I am a vegan. The eloquence with which the author explains his ethical choices is compelling to the point that I expect converts!"

—**Jeffrey Moussaieff Masson**, author, *Dogs Never Lie About Love* and
Beasts: What Animals Can Teach Us About the Origins of Good and Evil

"Kim's personal journey from slaughterhouse worker to dedicated and professional animal rights advocate is an interesting tale in itself. But it's his reflections on how we should put animal rights beliefs into effective practice which make *Growl* an especially valuable contribution to the growing body of Animal Studies."

—**Joyce D'Silva**, Ambassador, Compassion In World Farming

"Don't just read this book: underline sentences, highlight paragraphs, and take notes. That's what I did. Kim Stallwood is one of the sanest and most visionary leaders the animal rights movement has to offer. In this book, he has distilled forty years of wisdom gained from his own personal journey as an animal advocate on two continents and in various organizations. He explores the painful internal questions each of us asks ourselves as we struggle to be effective animal advocates in a world where animal exploitation is the norm. There are gems of insight in *Growl*, things that too often remain unsaid by animal activists, especially to each other. What I saw in this book is a mature and truly compassionate individual offering us signposts to becoming more skillful and holistic in our work on behalf of animals. Thank you, Kim; *Growl* left me purring."

—**Joyce Tischler**, Founder, Animal Legal Defense Fund

"Although every activist starts out on their own path to social justice, *Growl* showed me how much our thoughts and feelings are shared experiences. Both funny and philosophical, *Growl* is a joy to read and will be enjoyed by new and seasoned activists alike."

—**lauren Ornelas**, Founder/Executive Director,
Food Empowerment Project

"An erudite, engaging, and at times hilarious autobiography from one of the wisest voices of the animal rights movement."

—**Jonathan Balcombe**, biologist and author, *Pleasurable Kingdom*

"A fascinating read, not just for its personal account of one man's journey, but also for its history of the growth of the vegetarian/vegan/animal rights movement. I found a lot to identify with in the book: how hard it sometimes is to change people's hearts and minds; the scale of the task; how people rationalise away their treatment of animals and deny their responsibility; and how they eventually realise they must change. *Growl* is written from the heart and full of fascinating detail. I hope it's read not only by all who've renounced meat-eating and care deeply about animal rights, but by others who haven't yet embarked on that journey, but who will, I am sure, find the book's arguments compelling and persuasive."

—**Kerry McCarthy**, Labour MP for Bristol East

"A well-written read that is thoughtful, honest, and insightful."

—**Lisa Kemmerer**, author, *Animals and World Religions*, and associate professor at Montana State University Billings

"In *Growl*, Stallwood tells a remarkably honest story of his transformation from being a strident, self-righteous, misanthropic animal activist to becoming a reflective, compassionate, non-violent voice for justice for all animals. Along the way, he shares important insights for developing self-respect and strategies for successful activism."

—**Professor Lori Gruen**, author, *Ethics and Animals*, and Coordinator, Wesleyan Animal Studies, Wesleyan University

"Kim Stallwood is one of my animal rights heroes. His *Growl* is a must read for anyone interested in how we treat other animals. He instills hope that everyone's hard work matters; but that we can do better in bringing animals into a human-dominated world and peacefully coexist with them. Indeed, it's a win–win situation for everyone. Buy multiple copies. Read one and share the others."

—**Marc Bekoff**, author, *The Emotional Lives of Animals*, and editor, *Ignoring Nature No More: The Case for Compassionate Conservation*

"*Growl* is much more than the autobiography of well-known animal advocate Kim Stallwood. He weaves a larger story about animal activism in which he makes a call for justice, compassion, truth, and nonviolence. *Growl* is a book that new activists should read. Long-time activists will also wish they had it when they were just starting out."

—**Margo DeMello**, Human–Animal Studies Program Director, Animals and Society Institute and author, *Animals and Society: An Introduction to Human–Animal Studies*

"Kim Stallwood's life as an animal advocate mirrors the progress, in theory and action, of a movement that is poised to change the world. He emerges from these pages as insightful, passionate, occasionally opinionated, and, most of all, deeply devoted to principles of compassion and nonviolence. If you want to know where the animal rights movement has been, and want to think about where it's headed, you would do well to read *Growl*."   —**Mariann Sullivan**, Program Director, Our Hen House

"Inspiring and insightful, *Growl* is an eloquent blend of history and hope. Both a personal narrative and a call to action, *Growl* considers what it means to care deeply about animals and is essential reading for anyone who wants to better understand the animal-protection movement—and their place in it."

—**Mark Hawthorne**, author, *Bleating Hearts: The Hidden World of Animal Suffering* and *Striking at the Roots: A Practical Guide to Animal Activism*

"If you have spent years growling about the way animals are treated, you'll find Kim Stallwood a well-informed, reflective, and companionable fellow-growler. *Growl* is a personal chronicle of the modern animal movement, written by someone who has been a part of it from the early 1970s, and has thought hard about what it will take for the movement to succeed in achieving its radical goals. I hope a new generation of activists will read it, absorb its wisdom, and continue the march towards animal liberation."

—**Professor Peter Singer**, Princeton University, author, *Animal Liberation* and *The Life You Can Save*

"No one ever said that caring about animals was easy, especially in a world where society has a long way to go before animal cruelty is a thing of the past. Being struck by the plight of others and wanting to do something to help can be a lonely place. For anyone starting down this road afresh, *Growl* is the perfect companion.

In his introduction, Stallwood declares this book the one he would have 'loved' to read when starting down the long and often confusing road of trying to make sense of man's relationship with animals. Through his own experiences, the author navigates the complex web of thoughts, emotions, and motivations that can buffet those who want to make the world a better place for animals and thereby people. He lays bare personal flaws with engaging honesty. He crystallises what it means to care deeply for others of a different species as well as our own.

Stallwood pours forty years of hard lessons into this synthesis of humane thought. *Growl* gives us a rare glimpse of life as one of the animal movement's most enduring leaders."

—**Philip Lymbery**, Chief Executive, Compassion In
World Farming and co-author, *Farmageddon*

"We can learn much from Kim Stallwood's new book, written by an insider who helped shape the animal rights movement in the past, and who aspires to continue to do so in the future."

—**Professor Tom Regan**, author, *Empty Cages*
and *The Case for Animal Rights*

"Both new and seasoned activists will learn and be inspired by Kim Stallwood's *Growl*. It's an important—and highly engaging—exploration of the strategies and values that lie at the heart of effective activism for animals. Packed with stories and insider insights from the author's four decades of experience within the animal rights movement, this book reads like a captivating history of that movement. And at the same time, it's a guide for anyone who wants to make a difference for animals."

—**Virginia Messina**, MPH, RD, co-author, *Never Too Late to Go Vegan*

GROWL

Life Lessons, Hard Truths, and Bold Strategies from an Animal Advocate

KIM STALLWOOD

Risa,
Thank you for doing all
you do for the animals.
Kim Stallwood
2014

LANTERN BOOKS • NEW YORK

A Division of Booklight, Inc.

2014
Lantern Books
128 Second Place
Brooklyn, NY 11231
www.lanternbooks.com

Cover design by Lawrence & Beavan www.landb.co.uk

LIBRARY OF CONGRESS CATALOGING-IN-PUBLICATION DATA

Stallwood, Kim W.
Growl : life lessons, hard truths, and bold strategies from an animal advocate /
Kim Stallwood.
pages cm
Includes bibliographical references and index.
ISBN 978-1-59056-396-0 (paperback : alk pbk.)—ISBN 978-1-59056-397-7 (ebook)
1. Stallwood, Kim W. 2. Animal rights activists—Great Britain—Biography.
3. Animal rights activists—United States—Biography. 4. Animal rights
movement—Great Britain. 5. Animal rights movement—United States.
6. British Union for the Abolition of Vivisection—History. 7. Animal rights—Great
Britain. 8. Animal rights—United States. I. Title.
HV4716.S82A3 2013
179'.3092—dc23
[B]
2013023740

Dedicated to you, because you can make a difference

Contents

Foreword

BRIAN MAY

I was honoured to be asked to write a foreword for Kim Stallwood's definitive book about the journey of men and women towards decency. Did I say 'definitive'? Yes, I believe this book is important enough to be essential reading for anyone who has begun to listen to what their conscience says, as regards how we, as humans, behave towards the other beings on Earth, whether human or nonhuman.

There is, in human evolution, a time for ideas to germinate and become powerful social movements for change. It is highly significant that Archbishop Desmond Tutu said, in a foreword he wrote for *The Global Guide to Animal Protection*,

> I have seen first-hand how injustice gets overlooked when the victims are powerless or vulnerable, when they have no one to speak up for them and no means of representing themselves to a higher authority. Animals are in precisely that position. Unless we are mindful of their interests and speak out loudly on their behalf, abuse and cruelty go unchallenged.

This, from Tutu, a man who spent most of his life fighting against injustice to blacks, women, and gays, is a signal that our sensibilities are growing up. It is a call to us all to stand up for what most of us believe is right, on a larger stage than ever before.

The fact that you are reading this foreword is probably an indication that you are already in that group of humans who feel profoundly uncomfortable with vast areas of our everyday treatment of animals, and would like to make a change. I count myself in that group. Yet, for most of our lives, busy and ambitious as we are, and concerned with providing for a growing family, we turn a blind eye to that inner dissatisfaction. How can we turn ourselves into an instrument for change towards decency in human behaviour?

Kim Stallwood's fascinating account of *his* ongoing journey towards this goal is the best answer to this question I have ever seen. Although Kim is modest and self-critical, his life has already inspired many of us in our quest to give animals a voice. In this book, he chronicles his own passion as he makes a journey that is both real and symbolic, towards true decency. The only good parallel I can think of for his often painful honesty and sharp perception is John Bunyan in his *Pilgrim's Progress*. This book explodes many myths and bubbles; it levels all the high ground that many have believed they stood on, and plainly beckons us in humility and simplicity to a better way of thinking, in which we cause no unnecessary pain to any creature. Better than this, it opens the door to a world based on compassion, our greatest hope for us and our children, and our children's children.

Brian May

Dr Brian May, CBE, PhD FRAS, is a founding member of Queen, a world-renowned guitarist, songwriter, producer, and performer. He is also a Doctor of Astrophysics, 3D stereoscopic photographic authority, and a passionate advocate and campaigner for animal rights. He established the Save Me campaign (www.save-me.org.uk), named after his song, to champion all, but predominantly British, wildlife.

Introduction

Like many people who've been involved in social justice causes over several decades, I often wish that at the outset I'd possessed the strategic knowhow, the ability to communicate effectively, and other persuasive skills that I think I have now. *Growl* is the book I would have loved to have owned when I was a young man and I discovered how widespread was the cruelty we inflict on other animals.

The simple truth is that I couldn't have written it until now. I had to accrue from a lifetime of working for animals a deeper understanding of what caring profoundly about them truly meant. I needed to learn that, although we humans are capable of unimaginable malice towards other living beings, we can also be astonishingly kind. It was necessary to gain a comprehension of animal rights—and through that wisdom discover not only the transformative potential of kindness towards animals but how we need to apply that kindness to ourselves—to realise that although animal rights is, of course, about our relationship with nonhuman creatures, it's also about locating meaning in our lives and finding out who we truly are.

For almost four decades, I've worked at some of the world's foremost animal rights organisations in the United Kingdom and the United States. I've been intimately involved in the advance of the animal advocacy movement from the fringes of society to the main-stream. *Growl* is at once my first-hand account of that change, a reflection on the important lessons I've learnt, and an elucidation of the values I've come to believe must be at the centre of any effort towards implementing social justice—whether for human or nonhuman animals.

Growl is the story of an ordinary individual, very much a work-in-progress, who didn't undergo an immediate personal conversion when he discovered the horrors inflicted on animals. It's also about how I thought I had all of the answers to all of the questions about what was wrong with the world, yet I ignored vital issues about myself. In fact, my life seems more like a series of muddled chapters, missed as well as seized opportunities, slow realisations, and, of course, errors and misjudgements. *Growl* is, therefore, not so much a recollection in tranquillity of wisdom earned and lessons learnt but a report from a fellow soldier on the front lines of our common struggle for lives that matter—not for ourselves alone, but for those, regardless of species, whom we may never meet.

In grappling with challenges over the course of my life, I've come to believe that a commitment to animal rights requires an honest examination of our motivations in a never-ending process of engagement with others and a disciplining and opening up of our hearts to our frustrations and joys. Animals suffered when I set out to save them forty years ago, and they continue to do so today. A vegan is not completely innocent of animal exploitation; nor does he automatically become 'a good person', simply because he shuns all animal products. Veganism is not a destination so much as a journey: one that perhaps only highlights how confused and complex our relations with other animals are; one that aims to offer instead of rape, murder, war, cruelty, and environmental devastation, a little kindness, gentleness, and self-sacrifice en route.

I also believe that our commitment to animal rights must be animated by four key values:

- Compassion: our motivation for helping animals
- Truth: our ethical relations with animals
- Nonviolence: our value in the relations we have with animals
- Justice: our commitment to all animals

Not only are these principles more powerful in combination than singularly, but they're ones that most of us have already accepted for other members of our species (although perhaps only recently, and still only partially). These values, therefore, possess a certain strategic value, since they form a quartet that people who may not share our dedication to reducing animal suffering can understand. *Growl* explores these values in detail.

Before we continue, it's worth defining what I mean when I talk about 'animal suffering' or 'animal cruelty'. It should go without saying that all animal existence, of whatever species we belong to, involves pain and discomfort in the natural course of our lives. We're all going to die, and disease affects us all. Some animals are predators and some are prey, and I for one am not ready to deny the lion his right to hunt a gazelle, even though I may stop a domestic cat from trying to kill the birds in my garden.

In *Understanding Animal Abuse: A Sociological Analysis*, Clifton P. Flynn quotes sociologist Frank R. Ascione who defines animal cruelty as 'socially unacceptable behavior that intentionally causes unnecessary pain, suffering, or distress to and/or death of an animal.' Flynn notes that this definition excludes 'legal, socially acceptable behaviors (which are often deemed "necessary") that cause the most harm to animals—for example, factory farming, hunting, or animal experimentation'. He goes on to consider a definition of cruelty to companion animals written by Hannelie Vermeulen and Johannes S. J. Odendaal that describes more clearly what animal cruelty and exploitation *could* encompass. I've adapted their definition slightly so that it encompasses my understanding of all areas of animal use:

'[Animal abuse] is the intentional, malicious, or irresponsible, as well as unintentional or ignorant, infliction of physiological and/or psychological pain, suffering, deprivation, and the death of animals by humans' (96–97). This is what I mean when I talk about 'animal cruelty' or 'animal exploitation'.

I've spent most of my life growling about and against animal exploitation—thus the title of this book. Nonetheless, biographical elements aside, *Growl* doesn't focus on animal exploitation in factory farms, nor highlight individual acts of cruelty. The book doesn't contain graphic descriptions of the torture of animals. Instead, my goal is to explore how a deeper understanding of animal rights can lead us to discover what it means to be genuinely *humane*—by which I mean not merely kind to members of our own species, but caring towards other animals as well, in a compassionate, honest, peaceful, and just world. As the definition of 'animal cruelty' above suggests, I'm most interested in our attitudes—whether we're conscious of them or not—that cause us to harm others, and in presenting a way of being in the world that doesn't involve exploitation or abuse.

For some, the aspirations laid out in this book may seem pie-in-the-sky day-dreaming, the kind of optimism that no one can deny is a wonderful goal because no one believes it's achievable. Yet every engagement we make in the world draws on social, cultural, political, and economic norms that function individually and institutionally to guide our action and attitude. As adults, we're responsible for our behaviour and have a certain duty as informed citizens to understand how we impact the lives of others. In that regard, social transformation may be as simple, and as complex, as becoming conscious of one's world and one's behaviour in it.

Furthermore, to ignore the utopian vision altogether is to condemn ourselves to despair. Even though the aspiration to live with compassion, honesty, peace, and justice may seem impossibly idealistic, imagine what it would be like to inhabit a world entirely defined by their opposites: indifference, lies, violence, and injustice! This book argues that there is—indeed, *has* to be—another way to engage with the nonhuman world. No matter what others may say about what we do, we are answerable to no one else but ourselves. We may not be able to save the world. But we can save the world that is ours.

I

TRUTH AND COMPASSION

*Lies will flow from my lips, but there may perhaps be some truth mixed
up with them; it is for you to seek out this truth and to decide whether
any part of it is worth keeping. If not, you will of course throw the whole
of it into the wastepaper basket and forget all about it.*

—VIRGINIA WOOLF, *A ROOM OF ONE'S OWN*

*Here came the sun—an illimitable rapture of joy, embracing every
flower, every leaf. Then in compassion it withdrew, covering its face, as if
it forbore to look on human suffering.*

—VIRGINIA WOOLF, *BETWEEN THE ACTS*

1

From Camberley Kate to the Slaughterhouse

I was born in 1955, in Camberley, a small town in the county of Surrey, about thirty miles southwest of London, England. Camberley is home to the Royal Military Academy Sandhurst, which is a college for officers who want to serve in the British army. Royalty from Britain and around the world have attended the school over the decades. My family had lived in the area since the mid-nineteenth century, when John Stallwood, a boot maker, moved to the town to make footwear for the military trainees and officers. In 1851, he was the first to be interred at St. Michael's Church, which sits on land given by the military academy to the Church of England.

In the 1960s, my parents often took my sister, Wendy, and me to Camberley's main street on Saturday afternoons for the week's grocery shopping. We would frequently come across a small woman with glasses and unkempt, white hair tucked under a black beret, walking her dogs. Her name was Katherine Ward, and she was known as 'Camberley Kate'. I don't recall my parents telling me much about her, yet she was a source of fascination to me. Although I was slightly scared of her, she planted in my young heart a seed of compassion towards animals and an understanding of the importance of helping others that have flourished for half a century.

By the time I encountered Kate, she was a fixture in Camberley. Almost every day throughout the 1950s and 1960s, she left her modest home and walked a mile or two to the town centre, pushing a homemade wooden cart, which was coloured green. A sign painted in white on the front proudly declared, WARD STRAY DOGS. Inside the cart were small, sick, or elderly dogs; alongside trotted a further dozen or so larger hounds attached to the cart by leashes, string, or rope. The cart contained a small shovel to pick up anything the dogs left behind. Kate controlled her pack by employing a whistle and a fierceness that she wasn't afraid to use on anyone who ridiculed her.

Camberley Kate Ward. *Ronald Dumont/Hulton Archive/Getty Images*

No one knows who first called her 'Camberley Kate', but the nickname is the title of an article about her by historian Sir Arthur Bryant (1899–1985) published in the *Illustrated London News* in 1964 and collected in his anthology of essays, *The Lion and the Unicorn*. Bryant relates that Kate was born in Middlesborough, northeast England, on June 13, 1895. Both her parents died before she was ten, so she was raised by a very religious aunt in what she would later describe as an 'atmosphere of disapproval'. At nineteen, she left home to go into domestic service in Bradford, West Yorkshire. In 1943, she paid £600 for a Victorian working-class cottage at 218 London Road, in York Town near Camberley. Her work with animals started when she took home a lame greyhound, whom she found sitting on the doorstep of the local veterinarian's office and who'd been due to be euthanised. No longer working as a maid, Kate was now free to help dogs: 'You never had any time for that sort of thing [dog rescue] as a domestic servant in those days', she said.

Soon enough, people began to deposit dogs on her doorstep, sometimes in shopping bags or tied with string to the knob of her front door. Some were left with a note that stated they'd be left for 'just for a week', but no one returned to claim them. Others were dumped with her permanently because no one could look after them. The police also brought them and, mysteriously and miraculously, some found their own way to her. No dog was ever turned away.

Camberley Kate's meagre state pension didn't meet the costs of feeding and caring for so many animals. However, as she became more widely known, she began to receive donations. In his introduction to his essay on Camberley Kate, Sir Arthur Bryant notes that his original article raised 'more than £3,000 in spontaneous gifts' (178). Kate was often in the local and national press and on television programmes, including internationally on NBC in the United States and throughout Europe. She was recognised by *Dog's Life* magazine in 1967. In October of the following year, the documentary filmmaker Desmond Wilcox and Antony Armstrong-Jones (1st Earl of Snowdon and Princess Margaret's husband, and an acclaimed photographer) shot a film for television about people's relationships with animals, in which Camberley Kate was featured.

Fame didn't change her: her dogs always came first. She preferred them to people, she said. She placed any unused donations in a trust, as she didn't want to benefit personally from the animals in her care.

'I can only do a tiny bit,' Kate wrote to Bryant, 'over three hundred saved, and now at 69 years with only my old age pension I will spend my last years in taking, caring [for] and loving them' (180). She was still looking after as many as thirty-four dogs when she was in her early eighties.

Bryant wrote that Camberley Kate described herself simply as 'a Yorkshire lass that has the guts left to love the unwanted'. Bryant, however, saw in her something more. For him, she was the embodiment of what he understood Christian values to be:

> Obeying Christ's precept to *take no thought for your life, what ye shall eat or what ye shall drink*, this valiant and tender-hearted woman, because she loves, understands and pities these gentle, affectionate beasts betrayed and abandoned by man, shares with them her home and food, refusing none that are brought to her door, keeping them till she can find them homes and, in the meantime, trusting that somehow Heaven will provide for them. (179, italics in original)

A local veterinarian, Geoffrey Craddock, regularly visited her from 1954 until her death in August 1979, aged eighty-four. 'All the dogs were incredibly healthy and they lived to a ripe old age', he recalled. 'She had great humour, great character and great determination. I shall miss her very much indeed.' Camberley's Baptist minister, Reverend Christopher Russell, told *The Camberley News* after she died that Kate 'was an incredibly generous person on the quiet—she just gave and gave and gave to hospitals, charities, and churches.' He reiterated that, despite rumours to the contrary, Kate was not a wealthy woman: 'She just gave away every penny she had.' Indeed, she ensured that her donations were kept anonymous by making them through third parties. She also spoke of a 'gentleman' who helped to pay her expenses. When she died, Kate left her home and bank account to her remaining seven dogs, who were living in nearby kennels.

Kate's indomitable spirit and flair for publicity ensured that she couldn't be ignored—and nor could her concerns. In 1969, she fought against a proposed local law requiring dogs to be kept on a leash when they were outside. 'The Council is nothing more than a collection of dog-haters. I think this will be rotten. It means that dogs will be chained up all day', she wrote in *The Camberley News*. She also protested an attempt to prohibit dogs from the town's new shopping district. She wasn't afraid of authority, either. She wrote to King George VI to complain about a local hunting group losing control of their pack of dogs. When Princess Elizabeth married Prince Philip in 1947, Kate sent the bride and groom a dog leash as a present.

Kate had her detractors. They complained about the number of dogs she cared for and how she lived. Her eccentric behaviour didn't help. She reportedly confronted people taking her photograph because she had her own postcards to sell and she didn't like the competition. Local police recommended a route so that she and her canine entourage could leave and return home safely. Whenever she pushed her wooden cart against the one-way traffic along the High Street, she attracted a crowd of onlookers, including one small boy.

In her ordinariness and indeed her orneriness; in her relishing of the limelight and yet her quiet and self-denying generosity; in her visibility at the literal centre of town life and her invisibility at the margins of society; in her singularity and her spinsterish singleness; in her identification with her working-class roots and indifference to the powers-that-be that she nonetheless ensured couldn't ignore her, and which indeed occasionally celebrated her; and in her domestic servitude and as a servant to no one but the animals she loved, Camberley Kate embodies in microcosm the contradictions that are found in so many of the ways we see animals and those who advocate for them.

She was a woman who outspokenly preferred the company of animals to humans, and yet (without telling anyone) gave what little money she had to help the human poor and sick: Did she confirm or overturn the stereotype of the animal lover as misanthrope? Was she the crazy and sad dog lady who compensated for a lack of human companionship by taking in these animals, or was she the useful salve for the guilty consciences of those who couldn't be bothered to be inconvenienced by the dogs they'd acquired—a woman who knew fully the joys and responsibilities of many relationships? Was she the example of a failure of society to look after the displaced, disposable, and undesirable, or did she epitomise the self-abnegation we're all capable of in giving our lives over to the discarded and unwanted? Would she have been considered less saintly and more eccentric if she'd decided to look after animals we consume as opposed to 'man's best friend'? And if she had, what would that have said about how 'correctly' or otherwise we apportion our concern among the different species? Is it appropriate to praise her for her conforming to the Christian notion of sanctity in that her charity was selfless, but to ignore her non-politicised stance over society's continual abuse and discarding of billions of domesticated and farmed animals?

The answer, of course, is that she embodied all these contradictions, and many more, and we'll have reason to return to Camberley Kate often throughout this book. Nonetheless, whatever she might signify sociologically or politically when we talk about 'animal advocacy', I consider it an incredible gift—disturbing, strange, and unlooked-for though it might have been—to have been able to see Camberley Kate, even when I couldn't have imagined how much she would influence the course of my life.

Camberley Kate's seed of compassion did not fall on infertile ground. Although I wouldn't have been able to articulate any connection I might have to animals as a child, my parents always encouraged Wendy and me to be kind to them. My mother had wanted to work with animals but hadn't had the opportunity. I recall my father bringing home a small grey kitten soon after I was born. Tinkerbell's passing when I was about twelve was my first exposure to death.

By the time I was eleven, I'd joined the Royal Society for the Prevention of Cruelty to Animals (RSPCA), an act that required my recital in front of the headmistress of my school of an anticruelty pledge printed on a small, white membership card. Later, at my junior school, which is roughly comparable to an elementary school in the United States, my class was taken on a day trip to Brighton's dolphinarium. I looked down from a balcony onto what must have been an aboveground swimming pool, which cannot have been that large. I watched as an adult and baby dolphin swam in endless circles, the infant keeping close to the side of what may or may not have been her mother. I was horrified. Even at this young age, I could see that the confinement was cruel, but I was too young to know what to do about it. I remember that it seemed wrong partly because the dolphinarium was on Brighton's seafront. I couldn't imagine how it might feel to be so near yet so far from your own world. I was also disturbed by my biology classes, which included the dissection of a frog and watching a film that showed the live insides of a pig as her digestive system processed food over a period of twenty-four hours.

One more childhood memory about animals remains vivid, even though when I look back on it I failed to make an association at the time between the meat I ate and the dead animal it came from. I recall biting down on some gristle when my family was eating lunch. I cannot recollect what type of meat it was, but the physical sensation, the visceral impact of the gristle between my teeth as I tried to chew and swallow it, will never leave me. To this day, I avoid food cooked with vegan fake meat because it reminds me of this moment. Nevertheless, throughout the remainder of my youth I continued to consume meat, although I preferred the taste of chicken and fish to beef and pork.

UPSTAIRS AND DOWNSTAIRS

In my teens, my ambition was to become a chef and eventually to learn how to run hotels and restaurants. In spite of my distaste at eating gristle, I nonetheless enjoyed a wide variety of food—even to the extent of trying every other type of meat I came across, including frogs' legs. I appreciated the creativity involved in preparing food. I relished the hands-on care and attention required in gathering the utensils and chopping and mixing the ingredients. I liked moving around a well-stocked kitchen and opening a cookbook and choosing a recipe. I loved how my senses were stimulated as the ingredients were transformed through my skill and the mysterious alchemy that is cooking into the sizzling, roasted, or baked dishes that, in addition to sustenance, evoked the warmth of conviviality and the comforts of the hearth. I even took pleasure in the fact that—like a Tibetan sand mandala, which is thrown away once it's been painstakingly constructed—the success of my efforts in the kitchen was measured by how quickly the food was eaten and how little remained as evidence of the time, craft, and dedication I'd put into creating it.

Whereas other kids might have been excited about pop singers or movie stars, my idols when I was in my early teens were Fanny and Johnnie Cradock, who over two decades on British television were responsible for making cooking glamorous and sophisticated—two words that probably had never been applied to British cuisine before. So enthusiastic was I about them that at about the age of twelve I even saw their stage show when it came to Camberley. Food was also a way for me to escape the dreary British winters: I would read Elizabeth David's cookbooks to get a literal and metaphorical taste of life in the Mediterranean, something I could only imagine, since I'd never left England.

In spite of my love of cooking, I nonetheless found preparing and consuming beef, pork, and mutton unappealing and, at times, even nauseating, I didn't feel the same way about cooking and eating fish and chicken. Perhaps it was because their flesh appeared to be less meat-like, as it were—less bloody, veined, and fatty. Obviously, as I was to discover in a few years, being squeamish about certain forms of animal bodies and relishing others was illogical and inconsistent. But, like many people, I was able to hold seemingly contradictory positions at the same time and compartmentalise my concern for one and indifference to the other. Perhaps because resolving this discrepancy proved too difficult, I found that my greatest interest in food tended towards the delights of pastries and baking.

Mum and I before we were vegans. *Richard Stallwood*

I first came across veganism during what were then called Domestic Science classes, which I took at my secondary school. The teacher described vegans as people who were strict vegetarians, eschewing eggs and all dairy products. They were frequently nudists, she said (an assertion I've never cared to explore). Perhaps because of the clothing-optional association, my teacher's introduction to veganism left me cold. I continued to cook and eat meat, eggs, and dairy products.

At the age of sixteen, in 1971, I began a three-year course in French cuisine and hotel and restaurant management at Westminster College in Vincent Square, London. The college, now called Westminster Kingsway College, recently gained media attention because TV celebrity chef Jamie Oliver is also a graduate. During the summer vacations I was expected to work in the profession, and lecturers would help students get jobs through their contacts. The summer of 1972 found me employed in the pastry kitchen at Le Caprice, an haute-cuisine French restaurant near the Ritz Hotel on Piccadilly in central London. One of my most disturbing memories of working there was watching a chef cook rainbow trout. He grabbed a live fish from a nearby tank, whacked her against the side of the stove, and threw the stunned animal into a hot frying pan. Later, I learnt that the name 'rainbow' comes from the distinctive colours the fish turns as she is seared alive.

Another unsettling recollection from Le Caprice is of the pastry chef removing his underpants at the beginning of his shift, washing them in the pastry sink, and hanging them on the oven rail to dry. Unencumbered under his uniform, the chef then obviously felt free to create his delicious pastries, which were served upstairs to rich and important people in the ornate restaurant. By the end of the day, the by-now drunk chef would put on his now-dried underpants and go home.

Of course, the eccentric, temperamental, and egomaniacal culinary *artiste* is something of a cliché, as is the image of those 'downstairs' sweating and toiling in an unhygienic kitchen over the elaborate dishes that the aristocracy—the 'upstairs'—eat without much consideration or thought as to how the food and drink came to arrive on their immaculate bone-china plates or in their polished crystal glasses. But clichés become so for a reason: the stark contrast between the hot, squalid, and tempestuous kitchen and the glamorous and exclusive restaurant affirmed for me an essential division between the labouring and consumer classes that I'd noticed as a child. This division had coalesced throughout my adolescence into a conviction that the social order embedded unfairness, stultified ambition, and inhibited opportunity. As represented by Le Caprice, upstairs was languid, opulent, entitled, and powerful; downstairs was impoverished, feverish, and powerless. A first-class chef could afford to be capricious, and the diners might enjoy whimsy, but they had options and doors that opened up endless horizons beyond Le Caprice. Those who worked downstairs had their prospects limited by the four basement walls of their need for work, no matter how poorly paid or backbreaking it might be.

The expectations of what one could or couldn't do as a member of one's class affected everyone in Britain—although, as was the case with my family, it might not manifest itself in any particular political ideology. The aristocrat was in his own way as policed by his peers as the labourer was by his: how you talked, where you went, and with whom you consorted were rigidly if usually silently determined by your family, geography, social circle, and ultimately your own self-consciousness. I was raised in the council house I was born in, and all my schools were on the same estate. My maternal grandparents lived about a thousand yards away from us, and my paternal grandparents had a house only two or three miles from our own. Neither my father nor maternal grandfather had professional careers; my maternal grandmother was a cook at a local boarding school and my mother held various odd jobs around town. Apart from the occasional camping trip or caravanning holiday in the West Country, I didn't experience anything outside my nuclear family or my council-based world until I went to Westminster College at the age of sixteen. It's hard to imagine now, but throughout my childhood London was only a sixty-minute train ride away, and yet we rarely went there.

I performed well on my exams and during my fifteen minutes with a career guidance counsellor I was told I could do better than food and hotel management and should stay in school for my A-levels (the further qualifications that enable one to apply for university). However, I wanted to leave school and had my heart set on working in the food industry. I now regret not remaining and going to college or university. I believe I could have been a lawyer or academic, but my own stubbornness and perhaps a certain fear of risking the unknown beyond what was comfortable for me held me back. Ironically, my choice to leave school and pursue my interest would lead me within a few years to my life's vocation.

THE CHICKEN SLAUGHTERHOUSE

As the summer of 1973 approached, I decided against working in another restaurant. I assumed that I'd be doing this kind of work for the rest of my life, so I saw no compelling need to experience more of the same. Friends at other colleges and universities were taking jobs at a nearby chicken slaughterhouse, and since it paid well, would only last ten weeks, and I wanted to buy my first used car, it looked like an attractive option. I cooked and ate chickens without thinking about them, so why not work where they were slaughtered?

The abattoir was in Aldershot, Hampshire, a thirty-minute drive from Camberley. Like Sandhurst, Aldershot is a military town. Indeed, according to a sign you pass on entering, it's the Home of the British Army. I recall from an early age, when my parents would occasionally take Wendy and me shopping at the town's open-air market, that such boasting of military nationalism didn't sit well with my emerging political feelings—all part of an inchoate sense in me that violence only reinforced inequities instead of solving them. Aldershot's slaughterhouse was at the time one of the most advanced processing plants in the world. It employed eighty people and each week transformed 150,000 live chickens into pre-packed and frozen oven-ready birds. The slaughterhouse is now closed and the area is part of a small industrial site.

I worked on the post-slaughter section of the production line. The workers at the front end had to begin their jobs half an hour earlier than the rest of us because that's how long it took to hang a live chicken on the conveyor belt, kill and eviscerate her, run her body through the scalding tank to remove the feathers, and 'sanitise' the carcass. (Note: I say *her*, but both male and female chickens are raised and slaughtered for their flesh.) The odour of thousands of live birds fresh from the factory farm and the smell of their death hung over the plant and its environs.

I stood at my station with dead chickens approaching me on a conveyor belt every minute. The birds were neatly folded in preparation for the freezing process. It was my task for eight hours each day to place each carcass in a plastic bag (keeping the weight label in position), squeeze out the air in the bag, and twist and seal it by running it through a sticky-tape machine. I would then place the chicken on a large cart that was wheeled into a walk-in freezer.

I spent ten weeks that summer on the post-slaughter section of the production line, and I could never bring myself to watch the birds as they were killed. I also couldn't buy the oven-ready chickens that were offered for sale at a reduced rate as an employee benefit every Friday afternoon. Nonetheless, I continued to eat chicken bought elsewhere—naively believing that, because my plant wasn't where they were killed, I wasn't directly responsible for their death.

As these self-justifications illustrate, I was clearly uncomfortable at working at the slaughterhouse. Otherwise, I would have willingly bought the staff-discounted chickens and taken them home to cook and eat. Yet my compartmentalising and rationalising brain allowed me to justify my behaviour and pretend to myself that my ethics were consistent.

2

The Door Opens

Looking back, I can see how as I approached adulthood I was ready to change. My exposure to a wider world, my increasing unease at the existing social order, my discomfort with eating certain animals, and perhaps a need to define my own identity in some way—all these were to a greater or lesser extent leading me towards an adjustment in perspective. Like many of us who have a general feeling that something is wrong with the world around us and yet cannot pin down the source of that disquiet, an event or encounter with an individual is necessary for that shift to occur. I'd reached a point where there was no turning back on a journey of discovery into the disturbing side of human nature and what we do to animals.

If watching Camberley Kate pushing her wooden cart full of dogs with even more dogs in tow had awakened my feelings of compassion for animals, my experience of working in a slaughterhouse had exposed me to the shocking truth of animal exploitation. I began to ask myself, someone who was supposedly sensitive to the plight of animals, how it was possible that people like Kate Ward devoted their lives to rescuing dogs but I was willing to work to transform live chickens into food. I prided myself on my progressive political views—including opposition to war and violence—and my working-class origins. How could I justify my willingness to spend one summer employed in a slaughterhouse where violence was the norm and where my fellow workers lacked my options to move on? My rising concern for animals started to clash with my choice of a career that would include regularly cooking meat, eggs, and dairy.

In September 1973, I returned to Westminster College for my last year. I was anxious to meet up with my friend Amanda, who was in the year below me and the only vegetarian I knew. She was funny and hippyish, and I couldn't wait to be a macho man and try to upset her, even make her cry, at what I'd been doing. I was obviously so disturbed by the inherent contradictions in my consciousness that I was taking out on Amanda what I couldn't deal with in myself—and behaving in a way that was almost diametrically opposite to my true disposition.

Instead of being upset at my posturing, however, Amanda didn't bat an eyelid. Perhaps she saw my behaviour for the 'acting out' that it obviously was. For the rest of the year, Amanda and I argued back and forth about how or whether it was cruel to eat meat. I can't recall the details of our conversations, but no doubt I came up with all the stupid and self-serving reasons for why I should continue to eat animals that I would spend the next four decades countering. Thankfully, Amanda was unassuming and patient, and heard me out. Simply put, she won: Amanda convinced me that eating meat was wrong.

On January 1, 1974, my silly tough-guy nonsense stopped, and I became a vegetarian. Inconveniently, my course didn't end for six more months. How was I to cook and taste meat if I was a vegetarian? 'Fake it', Amanda said. '*Pretend* you tasted it.' Thankfully, I didn't have to 'fake it' that often. I asked my friends to taste-test the meat I prepared, and I completed the course with my newfound moral stance intact.

At the time, I was still living with my parents, although I enjoyed an active social life in London. When I told my mother I was now a vegetarian, her response was typical of many parents when faced with their child's newfound zeal: 'Not in my home, you're not!' Being a teenager of already strong opinions, I naturally interpreted her resistance as a fundamental challenge to my personal integrity. I was now an evangelising vegetarian—a vegelical! I believed she should be a vegetarian, too. I couldn't accept that she didn't see what I now saw.

In the early 1970s, my Domestic Science teacher's view of vegetarians (whether strict or not) was not unusual. Vegetarians were considered harmless oddballs and misfits. In fact, there was even a famous vegetarian restaurant in London called Cranks, which opened in Carnaby Street in 1961. At the time, all vegetarian foodstores were privately owned by well-meaning eccentrics—or so it appeared—who sold what were called *health foods*. I turned my snobbish haute-cuisine nose up at the rice, flour, margarine, and pasta that these places sold, since their food's colour spectrum seemed to range only from beige to taupe.

There were other inconveniences, too. Organic food had yet to make an impact on Britain and the health-food shop closest to Camberley was in a nearby village, and run by two elderly sisters. Even though the shop didn't offer very much, you could at least enjoy a cooked vegetarian snack at the couple of tables that huddled in the corner. I was glad and relieved when a year or so later Holland & Barrett, a national chain, opened in Camberley's new shopping centre. My mother would work there for several years. I always feel nostalgic whenever I visit Holland & Barrett because they continue to sell many of the same health-food products that I bought all those years ago.

After much heated debate between my mother and me about whether she should be a vegetarian, we agreed to a truce. She continued to cook meat-based meals for Dad, Wendy, and herself, but vegetarian food for me. Every Sunday, for example, she'd roast a chicken but cook the shop-bought sage-and-onion stuffing separately so I could eat it. Our knowledge of vegetarian nutrition was nonexistent, so my mother would add an egg to the stuffing mix to make sure I got enough protein. Mum was extremely accommodating to my dietary needs and she listened patiently to my opinionated outlook on the world.

Several months into my new regimen, I broke the truce. 'You should be a vegetarian', I said. 'You know you should be a vegetarian. Why aren't you a vegetarian?' To which she replied, 'When was the last time you saw me eat meat?'

She'd become a vegetarian but had never told me—wanting instead to see how long it would take me to notice. Self-absorbed and self-righteous young adult that I was, I hadn't paid enough attention to what my mother did or didn't eat. She remained a vegetarian, later becoming a vegan (as Dad did some years later), until her premature death from cancer in 1986. I joined the Vegetarian Society of the United Kingdom (VSUK), and Mum and I would read and study the newspaper it published for members. We also attended some meetings of VSUK's local branch.

Our beloved vegan cookbooks and Mum's handwritten recipes and clippings.
Paul Knight

My training in French cuisine helped with my transition to vegetarianism, particularly in its creative use of sauces and its refusal to boil every vegetable to death. I relied upon my beaten-up copy of *Practical Cookery* by Victor Ceserani and Ronald Kinton for ideas on vegetable dishes and salads. Our family's first vegetarian cookbooks included Rose Elliot's *Simply Delicious* and *Not Just a Load of Old Lentils*. Elliot would go on to become a prominent author of vegetarian and vegan cookbooks (indeed, one of my favourites is her *Complete Vegetarian Cookbook*). It made my culinary hopes rise when Elliot wrote in the preface to *Not Just a Load of Old Lentils* that '[v]egetarian cookery has a lot more to offer than dreary nut cutlets or lentil hotpot.'

As was often the case with vegetarian cookbooks of the 1970s and 1980s, recipes for dishes would include a lot of eggs, cheese, and milk—and Elliot's two early works were no exception. Our understanding then of what a vegetarian diet consisted was to imagine the traditional meat-and-two-veg meal without the animal flesh. My mother and I would make macaroni and cheese or, if we were ambitious, ratatouille! Comparing *Simply Delicious* and *Not Just a Load of Old Lentils* with an outstanding contemporary vegetarian cookbook such as Matthew Kenney's *Everyday Raw Express* is to see how far vegetarian cuisine has developed in the past forty or so years. Long gone are the defensive titles and apologetic descriptions. Increasingly, today's vegetarian cookbooks appear to be exclusively vegan or almost always include tips on how to replace all animal ingredients.

VEGAN PIONEERS

As 1975 came to a close, Mum and I agreed to phase out all dairy, eggs, and honey and try veganism from January 1. Later that month, we learnt about the BBC's innovative series of community-based television programmes called *Open Door*, and their decision to include the Vegan Society among the first. The programme was shown on

January 31, 1976, and again on February 7, and is available on You-Tube. After we watched it, we knew we'd made the right decision to go vegan.

To watch the show today is to be reminded how, nearly forty years on, many of the arguments made for veganism then remain the same today: that more people could be fed directly through plants than through animal protein, thus alleviating world hunger; that consuming dairy products involves more cruelty to animals than eating meat; that vegans lower their risk of contracting heart disease and cancers of the colon; that the vegan diet requires vitamin B_{12} supplementation (although this deficiency also occurs among many non-vegans); and that vegans are, according to one of the doctors interviewed, 'normal, healthy, happy people whom you couldn't distinguish from omnivores except that they are slimmer and perhaps smile more' [sic].

In the programme we meet two families who avow that vegan food is cheaper, no more time-consuming to prepare, and just as tasty as an omnivorous diet. They tell the interviewer they're providing their children with a nutritious, whole-foods-based diet and a set of ethical beliefs that will stand them in good stead should they choose to remain vegan later on. If anything dates the show, it's the naturopath who makes the case for veganism as a way to reduce the need for allopathic medicine.

As my mother and I watched the programme, we agreed that the Society's presenters had a point or two, but we thought the vegans on the programme were all rather, well, odd—paradoxically because they were so concerned to show themselves and their lifestyles as normal as well as natural. No one had shaved their head, or sported dreadlocks, or smoked or drank. No one wore bondage gear, tie-die, Birkenstocks, glam clothing, or other 'alternative' fashions of the times. No one talked of animals' souls or presented any outlandish spiritual beliefs. No one placed the suffering of the animals in the context of animal rights or the struggle for social justice (beyond complaining about how an omnivorous diet reduced the ability to feed the starving). No one advocated free love, communal living, or anarchy in the U.K. All wore clothes.

Instead, in their complete if stilted sentences, these white and imperturbably middle-class vegans offered their lifestyle as a wholesome, completely average existence for ordinary people—one profiled family were aptly named the Blands—who simply happened to dislike cruelty towards animals and thought animal agriculture was inefficient and environmentally unsound. An interviewee stressed that veganism was neither puritanical nor boring, but no one made it look particularly fun. Indeed, everyone appeared to have been told to be on their best behaviour—to resist emotion, stick to the facts, and act responsibly—even when extolling the benefits of their regimen. When one father observed that becoming a vegan was 'like shedding a very heavy, unwanted overcoat', the phrase seemed almost calculated to ensure the heart didn't race at the prospect.

Open Door was clearly original programming and an ambitious step for the Vegan Society to take. The BBC programme generated almost nine thousand inquiries and added about a thousand new members to the Society, including my mother and me. I subsequently got to know some of those who'd appeared on the show, such as Kathleen Jannaway (1915–2003) and Eva Batt (1908–1989). I discovered that they weren't odd at all, but actually dedicated pioneers—in many ways ahead of their time. Even though the assembled talking heads wouldn't have heard of climate change, let alone how methane and carbon-dioxide emissions from livestock exacerbate its effects, their arguments that intensive animal agriculture ruins the environment, that essential nutrients must return to the soil through composting, and that desertification should be combated through afforestation and reforestation speak directly and urgently to the environmental concerns of today. Even the beards on the faces of most of the men foreshadow contemporary back-to-the-land, hipster fashion.

Kathleen Jannaway, honorary secretary of the Vegan Society.
The Vegan Society

When she wasn't turning over the compost heap, Kathleen Jannaway was making a profound impact on many people through her decades of indefatigable work for the Society. She, like many in the programme, was a quintessentially English vegan—the personification of unflashy determination and a no-nonsense practicality that masked a passionate idealism. In *Animal Century*, Mark Gold describes how Kathleen met Jack Jannaway before World War II. They were pacifists and conscientious objectors:

> It was during the war that the couple turned vegetarian. At precisely the same moment as Kathleen was slicing up their meagre ration of roast lamb, there was 'a bit of a commotion in the corner of the field outside our window and all the lambs hastily raced for their mothers. I realised that it would be no good crying for mum when the slaughterhouse lorry arrived', she recalls. Both she and Jack decided never to eat meat again. (134)

I bought our first vegan cookbook from the Vegan Society: Eva Batt's *What's Cooking?* Inside my copy are slips of paper on which my mother wrote recipes for peanut loaf and rock cakes, and newspaper clippings with recipes for quick curry and bean-and-carrot soup by Rose Elliot. In my edition, Eva writes:

> These recipes are a selection of our 'first choice' meals and are planned for an economy budget. Economy need not mean dowdy meals, lack of flavour or low nutritive value. If the suggested ingredient is temporarily priced high—out of season or scarce—it can easily be replaced with a similar one available at the time. In any case, fruit and vegetables in season are preferred. If, conversely, a more glamorous dish is desired, it is a very simple matter to replace one vegetable for a more exotic one, aubergine, avocado, etc., or to add to it. Top a roast with slices of fried pineapple for instance or serve 'Delice' cream on the dessert. (v)

In addition to writing *What's Cooking?* and its sequel, *What Else Is Cooking?*, both published by the Vegan Society, Batt volunteered for the society from 1958 to 1982 on the management committee and as chair and honorary secretary. It's possible to see from her introduction to *What's Cooking?* how the Vegan Society drew from its origins in World War II and Quakerism and pacifism—including that of the founder, Donald Watson (1910–2005)—the stoicism, doggedness, and self-reliant spirit that characterised many British vegans in the post-war period, one that perhaps masked the quiet and profound radicalism at the heart of their message.

In November 1944, when victory over Nazism was far from certain, Watson published the first issue of *The Vegan News*—placing veganism within the context of the dissenting traditions of British social-reform movements extending back to the late eighteenth century:

> A common criticism is that the time is not yet ripe for our reform. Can time ever be ripe for any reform unless it is ripened by human determination? Did Wilberforce wait for the 'ripening' of time be-

fore he commenced his fight against slavery? Did Edwin Chadwick, Lord Shaftesbury, and Charles Kingsley wait for such a non-existent moment before trying to convince the great dead weight of public opinion that clean water and bathrooms would be an improvement? If they had declared their intention to poison everybody the opposition they met could hardly have been greater. There is an obvious danger in leaving the fulfilment of our ideals to posterity, for posterity may not have our ideals. Evolution can be retrogressive as well as progressive, indeed there seems always to be a strong gravitation the wrong way unless existing standards are guarded and new visions honoured. For this reason we have formed our Group, the first of its kind, we believe, in this or any other country.

In his statement, Watson was referring to the work of the anti–slave trade activist William Wilberforce (1759–1833); the philanthropist Lord Shaftesbury (1801–1885); the novelist Charles Kingsley (1819–1875); and the campaigner for improved sanitation Edwin Chadwick (1800–1890). Another lineage Watson might have evoked lay in the more radical and even atheist philosophies of the political novelist William Godwin (1756–1836), his wife and feminist pioneer Mary Wollstonecraft (1759–1797), their daughter Mary (1797–1851), and son-in-law Percy Bysshe Shelley (1792–1822), both of whom espoused vegetarianism for a while.

The social justice campaigns of the nineteenth century (e.g., ending the slave trade, slavery, and child labour; improving working conditions, prisons, poorhouses, and sanatoriums for the insane; extending the suffrage; and banning dogfighting and bear-baiting) were the focus of two approaches that were inherently in conflict: the conservative, ameliorist Christian tradition embodied by Wilberforce *et al.* and the more radical social reformers who campaigned for prohibition. This conflict between regulation and abolition has marked the history, ideologies, and visions of animal advocacy and vegetarianism/veganism in the English-speaking world ever since.

By 1824, the writings of, among others, the Anglican cleric Humphrey Primatt (1735–1776/7) (whose *A Dissertation on the Duty of Mercy and Sin of Cruelty to Brute Animals* was published in 1776) and the philosopher Jeremy Bentham (1748–1832), whose famous argument articulated in his *Introduction to the Principles of Morals and Legislation* was that the essential measure of our treatment of animals was not whether animals could talk or think but whether they could suffer, had brought cruelty towards animals to sufficient attention that that year a group of twenty-two influential men began the Society for the Prevention of Cruelty to Animals (SPCA).

The governing council of the SPCA formed two committees, which had the responsibility of encouraging kindness towards animals among the poor and inspecting working people's treatment of farmed animals at markets and in slaughterhouses. The all-male committees included Members of Parliament, Church of England clergymen, and such prominent anti-slavery campaigners as William Wilberforce. The patriarchal grip on the society's leadership was relaxed in 1829 when the council voted to establish a 'committee of ladies' to further its objectives, but it was short-lived and women were not permitted to serve on the SPCA's General Committee until the late 1880s (Moss, 1961, 24). In 1840, Queen Victoria's imprimatur consolidated the now *Royal* Society of Prevention of Cruelty to Animals' position at the centre of the British establishment and among the ruling elite.

The RSPCA was not solely set up to reduce cruelty to animals. As its programme clearly reveals, the founders were also motivated by *who* was being cruel. Britain, somewhat deservedly, has a reputation as a nation of animal lovers, but the RSPCA's origin reveals broader class, gender, and other biases and prejudices towards humans and other animals—something that has continued to this day. Some within the animal rights movement may claim that speciesism (roughly, the prejudice for one species over all others) exists on a continuum alongside sexism, classism, and racism, but the manner by which some advocates and organisations have campaigned—both in the past and present—reveals either no such commitment to moral consistency or convenient ignorance of it when it's expedient to do so.

It's hard to overstate how deeply embedded class consciousness has been in British animal advocacy—although it may not have been acknowledged by any side in the discussion of what the 'correct' treatment of which particular animal should be. In 1751, for instance, the satirist and artist William Hogarth (1697–1764) produced four printed engravings titled *The Four Stages of Cruelty.* In the first painting of the series, we see Tom Nero—a working-class orphan, who begins his descent into lawlessness as a teenager when he abuses a dog in the streets of London—surrounded by other varieties of animal cruelty taking place. In the second picture, Tom, now a coachman, viciously beats his horse when she collapses under the weight of a carriage she's pulling that's overloaded with four corpulent lawyers. The panel displays other beasts of burden being mistreated.

In the third engraving, Tom murders his pregnant lover after stealing from her employer. Nero only becomes a valued member of society when, in the fourth picture, his body is dissected by medical students after he's found guilty of murder and hanged. In an ironic and poignant reversal of the first picture, Hogarth depicts Nero's heart falling to the floor to be eaten by a skinny dog.

Aside from its sardonic reflection on the immorality of vivisection, Hogarth's engravings illustrate a phenomenon that contemporary sociologists and child-development specialists are now drawing to the attention of law enforcement and social workers: that a young person's harming of animals may be a displacement of abusive conditions at home and/or a prefiguration of violence towards humans when the child becomes an adult (Merz-Perez and Heide, 2004; Linzey, 2009). Once you set out on the path of cruelty, Hogarth suggests, the violence only increases until you yourself are its victim. The satirist also makes a political as well as moral point about the socially debasing effect of animal abuse. It's not that Tom is just inherently cruel, but his living conditions normalise cruelty; when everyone around you is an abuser, then no one is.

Hogarth's dystopian vision is located among the working and merchant classes of London, and reflects the concerns of clergy, politicians, and aristocracy at the time and later about the general lawlessness of the urban 'lower' classes when they indulged in such blood sports as bear-baiting and cock-fighting, and the gambling and excessive alcohol consumption that accompanied them. Such anti-social behaviour, they feared, might encourage riotousness and po-tentially social unrest. The British ruling class needed little reminder of the seismic social and political consequences for loyalist and mon-eyed interests that the American and French revolutions at the end of the eighteenth century had unleashed or the economic upheaval caused by the industrial revolution, which was emptying rural areas ('the shires') and forcing huge numbers of people into the cities in the first half of the nineteenth.

In 1835, parliament passed the Protection of Animals Act, which made bull-, bear-, and badger-baiting, as well as cock- and dogfight-ing illegal. Although the act was one of the world's first pieces of animal-welfare legislation, it covered cruelty only to domestic and captive animals and not wild ones—conveniently ignoring the hunt-ing of foxes, deer, and stags, all of which were pastimes of men of power and property. Unlike the behaviours that we see in Hogarth's *Four Stages of Cruelty*, horse-racing, grouse-shooting, sport-fishing, and riding after hounds were considered noble character-building pastimes and the training ground for the future leaders and lieuten-ants of the Empire.

In a similar vein, the RSPCA in 1882 initiated a humane education programme through its Bands of Mercy, which encouraged working- and middle-class children to read such books as Anna Sewell's *Black Beauty* (1877) and Margaret Marshall Saunders' *Beautiful Joe* (1893). These and other tracts were popular, depicting animals as sentient beings who deserved the respect of children and adults alike. The aim was to produce a civilising effect that would ensure compliance with and loyalty to the social status quo.

Of course, the prosecution of cruelty towards any animal and fostering kindness to them are laudable and essential activities. However, the RSPCA's prestige ensured that the society never strayed too far into such contentious issues as vegetarianism and vivisection. The former challenged the accepted orthodoxy on food production and who had power and control over the land, while the latter questioned the authority of the man of science, who by the latter half of the nineteenth century had recast himself as a respectable professional rather than the sadistic and incompetent mortician of *The Four Stages of Cruelty*'s final panel.

The work of advancing vegetarianism and ending animal experimentation was therefore left to others. Although the word 'vegetarian' was coined in 1842, the world's first vegetarian society wasn't founded until 1847, in England. The society undertook some initiatives throughout the 1800s, some secular and others spiritual, but none rivalled those of the RSPCA in their capacity to effect change, their access to power, and their social standing. It was the RSPCA that helped pass the Cruelty to Animals Act of 1876, the world's first law specifically to regulate animal experimentation and not replaced until the Animals (Scientific Procedures) Act of 1986.

VEGAN EVOLUTION

I didn't know any of this historical background when I saw the *Open Door* programme. Watching it again after all these years, I'm tempted to wonder what Donald Watson, Eva Batt, and Kathleen Jannaway would make of today's vegetarian personalities, such as the cookbook author Isa Chandra Moskowitz, *Sea Shepherd* captain and eco-warrior Paul Watson, and Johnny Marr, English guitarist, singer, and songwriter (with Morrissey) of The Smiths. In little more than two generations, animal advocacy and veganism have evolved from post–World War II pacifism, frugality, and stoicism to celebrities, cupcakes, and urban chic. The movements are more international and cosmopolitan, and while some may still associate veganism with virtuous self-denial, the diet has also acquired a certain glamour and notoriety.

At the same time, veganism is now so mainstream that a U.S. president (Bill Clinton) and vice president (Al Gore) can extol its virtues, and vegan options can be found in many restaurants and grocery stores in Europe and North America. A well-planned, healthy vegan diet is now recognised as 'nutritionally complete and healthy' by the National Health Service in the United Kingdom. And the American Dietetic Association considers veganism to be 'healthful, nutritionally adequate, and may provide health benefits in the prevention and treatment of certain diseases'.

I don't want to overstate the challenge Mum and I faced when we became vegan in 1976. Nevertheless, I wish we'd had access to what is so widely available today. Making life-affirming decisions of any kind is an important moment in anyone's existence, but I cannot help but think that the context of when we went vegan was very different and far more challenging than what appears to me to be the comparatively easy circumstances people have today.

I recall my first experiment—and I use this word deliberately!—with soymilk. Notwithstanding the bounty on display at the end of the *Open Door* programme, and the claims made by the vegans on the show that it was easy to make your own milk, the only available commercial nondairy milk was produced by Plamil, a company founded and still directed by vegans. Plamil soymilk came in a can in the mid-1970s. I poured the liquid contents into a jug and, as instructed on the label, filled the can with water and added it to the jug to dilute the milk to the correct consistency. Naively, I had the expectation that the liquid would taste and feel like cow's milk. Nothing could be further from the truth! Digestible it was not and so down the sinkhole it went. For the first decade or so of my vegan life, I didn't drink or cook with any form of milk.

The only place to buy tofu was in Chinatown in London's West End. After demonstrations or meetings, I'd often go to the Chinese supermarkets to buy blocks of tofu that floated in water in plastic bowls. Using the tongs provided, I'd carefully pick out the fragile white bricks and place them in plastic bags to take home. Visiting the Chinese supermarkets was an exercise in tunnel vision and nose pinching. Everywhere, it seemed, I saw pressed ducks hanging from hooks on walls, shelves, and in windows.

One soy product, however, stands out for me from the rest. It was a staple for vegan animal rights activists in the United Kingdom from the 1970s onward. Sosmix was a dried combination of textured soy protein and other ingredients to which you added cold water and shaped into sausages or burgers to fry. Sosmix was produced by Direct Foods, which the founders of Compassion In World Farming had set up. I remember no end of conversations among broke vegan animal activists about the different ways it could be cooked: such as baked in a pastry-crust pie or rolled in pastry to make vegan sausage rolls. Many a hunt saboteur started their morning with a Sosmix sausage sandwich.

During the two years I was a vegetarian, and then in the first year as a vegan, my involvement with Britain's animal welfare movement was as a supporter. The opportunity to become more involved as a full-time campaign organiser offered me hitherto unimaginable possibilities to learn more about how we treat animals. It also meant I had to confront the emotional and intellectual responses awareness of animal cruelty and exploitation inevitably caused.

3

The Commitment to Truth

Once I became a vegetarian, I knew what I *didn't* want to be part of, but I had little sense of what it meant to be an animal advocate. Before I write about my first tentative steps in the animal rights movement, I want to explore two fundamental values—truth and compassion—in the light of the psychological shift that I, and others, have undergone, in order to become animal advocates. It's my belief that a more rounded comprehension of just what it entails *psychologically* to become an animal advocate will enable those of us concerned with the suffering of animals to be more effective in the public sphere.

WHO ARE ANIMAL ADVOCATES?

In his book *Empty Cages*, American philosopher Tom Regan describes animal advocates as 'Norman Rockwell Americans' who stand for 'love of family and country, for human rights and justice, for human freedom and equality, for compassion and mercy, for peace and tolerance, for special concern for those with special needs (children, the enfeebled, the elderly, among others), for a clean, sustainable environment, for the rights of our children's children's children—our future generations' (19). (Norman Rockwell was a popular American painter and illustrator who depicted everyday life.)

Regan is being hyperbolic to make the point that animal rights is a revolutionary credo only in as much as, first, it is serious about the ethical mandate to care for the vulnerable and, secondly, that it takes abstract virtues at face value and not simply as political talking points. He wants to draw attention to animal rights as a *positive* moral code of behaviour and a realisation of pre-existing rights and responsibilities, wholly consistent with the American tradition of individual liberty, and not as some newfangled or foreign theory that aims to *remove* the rights of others to do as they wish.

Regan is also clearly concerned to present a rosy picture of animal advocates because of the prejudices that we've seen were applied to people like Camberley Kate. The vegans on the *Open Door* programme clearly had the same goal in mind. Regan wants to remind readers that we are not radical subversives or misanthropic loners but family folk and holders of values and interests that extend across the political spectrum as opposed to single-issue obsessives. In other words, animal advocacy is both normal and normative—an 'acceptable' attitude fully compatible with capitalism, patriotism, and a range of perfectly 'acceptable' social concerns, such as care for the environment or consideration for the less fortunate among us.

I understand the point that Regan is trying to make, and I've met many animal advocates who are teachers, nurses, social workers, parents, and volunteers of all sorts who are dedicated to making the world a better place for humans *and* animals. That spirit was alive in the vegans I saw on *Open Door*, and as we saw with Camberley

Kate it's sometimes present even in those whose outward behaviour would suggest a curdling of the milk of human kindness. Regan's characterisation also points to a truth that animal advocates *can* be found across the political spectrum. These days, it isn't as difficult to explain our passion and conviction to a non-committal audience as it was when I first started out.

However, as I'll argue later, I don't think it serves anyone's interest to sugarcoat what animal advocacy entails or to over-simplify the complex set of motivations and impulses of those of us who care deeply about how animals are treated.

But who are animal advocates? Regan describes three basic personality types: Davincians, whom he says feel intuitively for animals and are 'born with an ability to "enter into the mystery of the interior lives of animals"'; Damascans, who 'undergo a dramatic and often instantaneous perception change in their attitude toward animals'; and Muddlers, who 'grow into animal consciousness step by step, little by little' (21–25). At different times, he notes, we may be a combination of two or all three of these personae.

Psychologist Ken Shapiro adopts a different taxonomy. Animal advocates he suggests are 'caring sleuths', who 'persist in assertively and, when necessary, aggressively exposing animal suffering' (171). Caring sleuths see animal cruelty and exploitation when many others don't. A leather coat is not a glamorous accessory but the skin of a dead cow; the advocate would no more wear such a piece of clothing than she would one made from human skin. Visiting a zoo is not educational and entertaining but like touring a prison for the innocent. Shapiro places considerable emphasis on the quality and depth of caring experienced by animal advocates. 'It means being attentive to them [animals] in a watchful and concerned way', he writes. 'More than just a curiosity or interest, it is a positive inclining or leaning toward them, a sympathy for them and their needs. A caring attitude is one of continuous sensitivity and responsiveness, not a transitory awareness or a momentary concern' (157).

Caring deeply about animals may begin in childhood when we see something disturbing. Moral shocks—Regan's Damascene moment, named from the conversion of the apostle Paul on the road to Damascus (Acts 9:3–9)—sometimes occur as a confrontation between parents and friends and the circumstances in which they live. Like a candle that smoulders for years and suddenly burns brightly, so we may find sensitivities bursting into flame. The psychologist Manny Bernstein recalls, for example, falling off a tricycle as a young boy, after which a German shepherd dog licked his face to comfort him (153). Helen Jones, founder of the International Society for Animal Rights, was traumatised around the age of five when she and her mother visited a zoo. 'As we entered we saw a large white rabbit, transfixed with fear, in a cage with a snake', she wrote. 'Within a second or two the snake began swallowing the rabbit. . . . My mother never again entered a zoo. I did, many years later, only to collect evidence for a legal case' (Shapiro, 157). I, too, had my encounter at the dolphinarium.

For many people, the moral shock strikes at the heart of how they see themselves and their world. It's a personally transformative moment that hastens uncomfortable and hitherto hidden realisations. When my colleague Jill Howard Church and I interviewed Paul McCartney in his London office for the animal rights magazine I edited called *The Animals' Agenda*, the musician spoke of the moment when he and his then-wife, Linda (1941–1998), looked through the window of their Scottish home as they ate lamb and saw sheep outside. He recalled that Linda said, 'It's still got red blood. It doesn't bleed green blood, love. It's still just the same. It's got a face, and its mommy loves it. . . .' McCartney felt he was 'waking up' to an idea that meant breaking away from his own family's tradition and making his own way in life with Linda (Stallwood, 2001, 12–13).

The Animals' Agenda interview with Paul McCartney was published in 1998. *ASI*

A moral shock may also be prompted by the discovery of the connection between a beloved companion animal and other animals. Regan and his wife, Nancy, were grieving over the sudden death of their dog Gleco, who was accidentally killed by a car. At the time, Regan was researching Mahatma Gandhi (1869–1948) and pacifism, which had in turn introduced him to Gandhi's vegetarianism. Regan writes: 'My head had begun to grasp a moral truth that required a change in my behavior. Reason demanded that I become a vegetarian. But it was the death of our dog that awakened my heart. It was the sense of irrecoverable loss that added the power of feeling to the requirements of logic' (1987, 27).

As Shapiro notes of the caring sleuth: first, we care; then, we see; and then we seek out animal suffering. The 'provenance of suffering' must be revealed (Shapiro, 1994, 163). We shine a spotlight, refusing to conspire with the society hiding it from view. We want others to see what we now see, to experience similarly transformative moments. We believe society will change if enough people undergo enough moral shocks. That urgency is why the animal rights movement and its repertoire of protest (e.g., demonstrations, boycotts, civil disobedience, and publicity stunts) is so focused upon fomenting public outrage. The emphasis is on the individual to think, care, and act. Go vegan! Go cruelty-free! Don't buy fur! Boycott zoos! If I can change, you can, too!

When I worked in the chicken slaughterhouse, I saw institutionalised animal exploitation for the first time. In later years, I discovered even more ways in which animals are exploited by a complex of industries. The more I learnt, the more I needed to seek out animal cruelty and exploitation. As I discovered its pervasiveness, I had to learn how to cope with that knowledge. I had to reconcile myself with the truth that animals are being tortured and killed every second of every minute of every hour of every day, year in and year out, frequently for no other reason than momentary, gustatory pleasure.

The result for many of us who take on that knowledge is a strange, bifurcated existence. I live in my vegan world, in which I see what I think is food; and I live in a meat-eating universe. The same is the case with the leather furniture I may sit upon, the soap I may wash my hands with, or the gelatin capsules my medication may come in. In grappling with this psychic contradiction, psychologist Mary Lou Randour describes a day in the life of a woman she names Eve, who 'like many of us strives to be good and spiritually responsible, and to instill meaning in her life' (119). Randour depicts Eve's activities and contrasts them with how they impact the lives of animals. For example, Eve puts on a fur-trimmed parka to take her dog, Pepper, out for a walk: 'The coyote who was skinned for Eve's parka led a satisfying but uneventful life until the day he took a wrong turn and got caught in the steel jaws of a leg-hold trap' (125).

Amanda Pankiw speaks for me as well when she describes how

she began to see meat no longer as food but as 'raw flesh': '[O]ne day, I was doing my weekly grocery shopping. That week the store that I shopped at was having a meat sale. They gave the customers a big brown bag to fill up with meat and then the customer would get ten percent off. The sight of this made me sick to my stomach. A big bag of raw flesh. All of these people wheeling their carts around the store with bags of flesh in them. I quickly got the rest of the things I needed and got out of there' (Towns and Towns, 2001, 143).

Not surprisingly, perhaps, we caring sleuths find ourselves continuously torn by such a dichotomy. We do what we can personally to match our values with our life choices: we go vegan; stock our medicine cabinets and closets with cruelty-free products; and avoid leather, wool, silk, etc. We volunteer at the local shelter, foster stray animals, and patronise companies that are vegan or promote animal rights. But more than that, we feel obliged to stay in the moment of animal suffering—notwithstanding its emotional and psychological toll. To leave is impossible. It would be to abandon the animals. This is something we cannot do. If we're not there, who will be? *We* must care because no one else does. *We* must act because no one else will. *We* must remain true in spite of the ridicule, the dismissals, and the condescension. *We* must be permanently on call to respond to the demands of our conscience.

These are the first truths of animal advocacy: that what society considers usual is obscene; that the normative 'truth' about what is ethical to do to animals is in fact an 'untruth'. As historian Keith Thomas notes, society's relationship with animals is built on a 'mixture of compromise and concealment' (303). The concealment is itself an untruth, in that we name food to hide its true source. A dead pig becomes 'pork', an infant calf becomes 'veal', and 'meat' is not identified as the charred remains of a dead animal but as a delicious and nutritious—even ethical—centre for the plate.

The feminist philosopher Carol J. Adams calls the beings who become these euphemisms 'terminal animals'. She writes:

Terminal animals suffer literal constraints upon their freedom: most are unable to walk, to breathe clean air, to stretch their wings, to root in the dirt, to peck for food, to suckle their young, to avoid having their sexuality abused. Whether warehoused or not, all are killed. They are not able to do something which is important for them to do, and they lack the ability to determine for themselves their own actions. (1994, 118)

The words 'terminal' and 'animal industrial complex' here describe not merely the mechanised denial of every aspect of what it means to be alive, but they starkly draw attention to the inescapability, the absolute trappedness within a literally de-animating environment, for these creatures. These animals are defined by the violence we do to them. Their days are numbered from before they're born until they're killed. They have no other destiny than as our products or services.

The pervasiveness and totality of that world of animal rearing and slaughter delineate the 'animal industrial complex'. The term was first explored by the anthropologist Barbara Noske in her book *Humans and Other Animals*, although my preferred definition is by the sociologist Richard Twine, who describes it in an article entitled 'The Industrialisation of Animals: What Happened to Ethics?' on *The Scavenger* website. He calls it a 'partially opaque network of relations between governments, public and private science, and the corporate agricultural sector. Within the three nodes of the complex are multiple intersecting levels and it is sustained by an ideology that naturalises the human as a consumer of other animals. It encompasses an extraordinary [sic] wide range of practices, technologies, identities and markets'.

The animal industrial complex needs *power* and *control* to maintain its existence. Both are based on a belief that the subject to be controlled possesses no rights of any kind. Animals are considered property under the law, which ensures, as sociologist Clifton P. Flynn states, that animals are always open to the abuse of those who claim ownership of them (25–26).

The legal standing (or lack thereof) of animals and their economic status as disposable commodities legitimise the multiple institutions and manners in and by which we exploit animals for our use. In agriculture alone, each year the United States kills for food 8 billion chickens, 232 million turkeys, 103 million pigs, 30 million cows, 22 million ducks, and two million sheep and lambs. Globally, the world sucks 14 billion finned fish and 40 billion shellfish from the oceans or aqua-farms to eat, while hunters on an annual basis decimate at least 35 million mourning doves, 27 million squirrels, 17 million ducks, 13 million rabbits, 12 million grouse, quail, and partridges, six million deer, and thousands of bears, moose, elk, swans, cougars, turkeys, wolves, coyotes, and other creatures (Markarian, 2002, 91). Even our beloved cats and dogs are not immune from our carelessness with their lives. Six to eight million of them enter our public and private shelters, and three to four million of them are euthanised. Another 126.9 million animals are used in research laboratories throughout the world (Knight, 2011, 10–11).

These numbers constitute another set of truths: the ubiquity of our exploitation of other animals and the entrenchment of the mechanisms of evisceration within our society. It's hard to reconcile the scale of this slaughter when it is *actually born out of, and justified by*, the notion that our species is superior to all others. Yet, as my experience at the abattoir showed me, at some level we all know something is wrong with such systemic and systematic killing. Why else would we make sure in the United States that chickens are exempt from the U.S. Federal Humane Slaughter Act and rats (and birds and mice) from the U.S. Federal Animal Welfare Act? There can be no better symbol of the alienated status of animals from public policy and the law than the chicken locked away in a battery cage and the rat in a laboratory. How convenient it is to our consciences that the animals that we exploit in the largest numbers aren't under the law even considered 'animals' to whom it is possible to be cruel!

We've constructed a system for treating animals that depends on not being able to see inside the factory farms or slaughterhouses or research laboratories. If we did, perhaps we might not be as willing to eat fried chicken or take medication without first considering the consequences of our actions and their impact on people, animals, and the environment. The animal industrial complex is a gruesome gulag, involved in the imprisonment and extinction of beings far exceeding the worst atrocities we've committed on ourselves. The anonymous mass of creatures meeting the electric prod, the knife on the disassembly line, the stereotaxic restraint, or other forms of torture and death make it hard to comprehend the individual's suffering—yet each animal undergoes their own painful existence and dies their solitary death. As Mark Hawthorne notes in *Bleating Hearts*, these are forms of animal exploitation that do 'not get enough (or any) attention' (4).

A more immediate way to grasp the orgy of violence is to do a body count on *us*. The average meat-eater in the U.S. is responsible each year for the deaths of an eighth of a cow, a third of a pig, five-sixths of a turkey, 25½ chickens, 43 finned fish, and 134 shellfish. It surely says a great deal about our gluttony that we're willing to consume so many animals; our vanity that we drape ourselves with fur or leather; our pride when we order the rarest of steaks to exemplify our wealth or how manly we are; our cowardice when we shoot a white-tailed deer to show how strong we are; or our desire for control when we clone sheep or beat our dogs.

In order to escape from the truth of what we do, we tell untruths to ourselves and our children about the animals whose lives we abuse and take: that animals wouldn't exist or they'd overrun us if we didn't eat them, and that they're humanely slaughtered; that foxes like being hunted and that animals in zoos are often healthier than those in the wild; that elephants enjoy travelling from town to town and performing tricks in a circus ring; that animals surrender their lives to feed and clothe us; that only healthy chickens lay eggs in battery cages; that we need to drink milk for strong bones.

How ready we are to accept these and many other lies about how we couldn't survive unless we exploited animals! Most of us would be appalled at being considered a party to murder on such a mass scale, when we've never directly harmed or killed an animal in our lives. Indeed, it's beyond our comprehension that we'd ever do so. But this is what we do when we eat meat, eggs, and dairy or use cosmetics and household cleaning products or wear leather or fur.

The opening to the truth that accompanies the refusal to accept the lies about what we've been told about animals and our proper relation to them constitutes *in and of itself* a moral shock, as hitherto unimaginable ways by which animals are treated and exploited reveal themselves to us. The veil of secrecy is lifted. We discover that animal cruelty is present throughout our world, in the lives we live, the products we buy, and where we work and play.

The categories of Davincian, Damascan, Muddler, and the Caring Sleuth are stages we may go through, often more than once, perhaps simultaneously, and in no particular order. Each animal advocate tries to make sense of living in a world seemingly addicted to animal cruelty and exploitation. The characterisations help us to understand why, although Regan's original schema may say otherwise, animal advocates are not all the same and why we hold different and competing views about how animal rights and social justice can be achieved.

BLOCKED VEGETARIANS

The second set of truths that animal advocates are forced to confront is that no one ever promised that caring deeply about animals would be easy. No one could have reasonably believed that society could transform itself as quickly as we personally may have changed. To advocate for the rights of animals not to be eaten by human beings is to alter a mindset reinforced over thousands of years and countless generations. Eating meat is a comfortable, reassuring tradition valourised institutionally, theologically, politically, and economically.

Here, as with Regan's characterisation of vegans, it's possible to look at the glass half-full. In her book *Living Among Meat Eaters*, Carol J. Adams makes the case that vegans should view non-vegans as 'blocked vegetarians and their reactions to you as their symptoms of being blocked' (2001, 15). It certainly would appear that I myself was a blocked vegetarian when I fell into conversation with my college friend Amanda about her diet.

Adams further suggests that some non-vegans often react with such hostility to vegans around them, and that consequently we should label them *saboteurs*. Why do non-vegans think they have the right to treat animal advocates as the moral and psychological enema for their uneasy and defensive feelings about the dead animals on their plates? Why do non-vegans assume vegans have to be patient and listen to them as they prevaricate or struggle with giving up cruel and inessential animal products?

We are not obliged to be infinitely forgiving and affirming.

For the third truth that animal advocates need to face is that, in my experience, not everyone reacts to moral shocks as they could or, we might hope, should. Some never respond. They don't care about nonhuman animals and they never will. Instead, they make a virtue of their insensitivity.

THE MISANTHROPIC BUNKER

Confronted with a world of unremitting violence towards other animals, where others fail either to see what you witness everywhere or don't act on their own conscience, it's easy for advocates to seek refuge in what I call the 'Misanthropic Bunker'. We've all done it: no matter how positive or can-do our attitude about convincing others to become vegan or creating social change may be. And here is another truth about animal advocacy: that the retreat may be a necessary way of coping.

For some years, I've gone by the moniker of 'Grumpy Vegan', affecting a sort of curmudgeonly exterior that's partly a reaction to the fact that, in spite of decades of activism on my and others' behalf, animals are still being thoughtlessly mistreated, slaughtered, and eaten. Although I recognise that advocates have made progress in alerting people to the suffering of other animals, I'm painfully aware of how much more needs to be done. I fully confess to a settled melancholia about how limited are my abilities to bring about the end of the animal industrial complex. My grumpiness serves as a kind of protective skin that ensures that I make it through a day of exposure to human cruelty with my sanity intact.

Occasionally, however, I find myself drowning in the sea of blood. I turn for rescue, only to find those around me indifferent or even hostile. Even those I consider my colleagues in the struggle urge me to pull myself together and knuckle down because more work has to be done. *The animals don't have the luxury of waiting while you cope with your feelings*, they may say. *You cannot afford to feel weak for them.*

At moments such as this—when I'm overwhelmed, tired, and have lost confidence in myself that I'll ever achieve any meaningful change for animals—I retreat to the Misanthropic Bunker. I also do this when I'm fed up and disappointed with the animal rights movement. *We'll never achieve animal rights*, I tell myself. *Speciesism will never end. Animal rights will never be accomplished. It won't happen in my lifetime.*

Before you know it, the following spiel unwinds:

Why can't everyone care about animals like me? Why isn't everyone vegan? How can people go about their daily lives and not realise that they're killing animals all the time? It's all so obvious. I see animal cruelty everywhere. Why can't they?

I want to believe everyone will go vegan and embrace animal rights. But I know they won't. We don't care about animals enough. I'm not sure we ever will. Look at how we treat them! Throughout history, in every civilisation, people abused animals. Every minute of every day, some-where in the world, animals suffer. Nothing else matters.

Why don't more people like me experience the moral shock of ani-mal suffering? I know I wasn't born a vegetarian or vegan—I once ate meat—but nowadays it's never been easier. There's no excuse why not.

I don't understand how people can compartmentalise their thinking so that a vivisector can love their dog at home but go to work and ex-periment on dogs in a lab. But, then, I can't believe they truly love their family dog. How could they, considering how they make a living? What's more, how can we ever expect to be kind to animals when we can't even treat each other with respect? How can we ever expect to overcome such arrogance?

And so on. In such circumstances, it's hard to credit the doctor on the *Open Door* programme who noted that vegans seemed more likely to smile than omnivores. Positive attitudes, of course, have their place, and sunny optimists are more likely than dour pessimists to convince folks that their *modus vivendi* is attractive. But it's vital that animal advocates recognise that our work has costs. We need to grieve the loss of so much sentient life. We need to acknowledge our anger at human beings' unfathomable cruelty towards other be-ings and our species' irrational and self-serving responses to its own casuistry, thoughtlessness, and moral inconsistency. We need to ac-cept the reality that the world wasn't necessarily waiting for us—and only us—before deciding that it was going to become nonviolent and vegan. Sometimes a dark place within our soul is a good location within which we can safely express that rage, frustration, and, yes, despair at other members of *homo sapiens*.

I try not to lurk too long inside the Misanthropic Bunker. I know that for all the reassurance and sanctuary it provides as a place where it's possible to blow off steam and rail at how much better the planet would be without humans (unless those humans were like me!), it's also an excuse to wallow in self-righteous indignation. It's not only strategically vital to direct our animosities in a more positive and effective direction but it's also psychologically essential to avoid being consumed by hatred and intolerance. How we might go about doing this I discuss in the next chapter.

THE OAK TREE OF TRUTH

In this chapter, we've looked at a number of truths that confront the animal advocate, as well as the truths that can turn someone into an animal advocate in the first place. Before I explore the second essential component of animal activism—compassion—it's necessary to go a little more deeply into what might be thought of as a wider meaning of truth.

Imagine a mighty oak tree standing proudly in a beautiful green field. From afar, the tree is an organic whole. Standing underneath it, we can look into its canopy and see from its central trunk larger branches spreading outward, and smaller branches disappearing into the foliage. As we observe more closely, we perceive the uniqueness of each bough and every narrower limb. For all its individual components, nothing would be possible without the trunk. The branches couldn't grow if there was no trunk, for the branches ultimately all stem from that main trunk, and, in spite of their diversity, they share its characteristics. They are all equally interdependent.

This is how I envision universal truth—Truth with a capital 'T'. The tree in its totality is the universe; the trunk is universal truth; the large branches represent the world's religions and the smaller limbs their various offshoots and sects. Other branches symbolise different traditions in philosophy, and still others the different means (e.g., political, economic, and cultural) by which we try to make sense of the world.

We are the birds who live in the oak tree. Some of us stay on a main branch to build a nest to raise our young. Others of us range from offshoot to offshoot, exploring smaller limbs for a while before returning to the main branch. As we travel along boughs away from the trunk, we leave Truth to enter the localised truth of the world's various belief systems that offer a different and incomplete framing of Truth. Consequently, it's a partial version of Truth. This analogy helps to explain why the origins of the world's religions are so closely identified with specific regions of the globe, as well as the similarities and differences among them.

Just as it's hard from our perspective as tiny birds on the enormous oak to comprehend or experience the totality of the entire tree, so we tend to believe our boughs (our systems and sub-systems of beliefs and ideologies) are the entire Truth. The fragmented aspects of universal truth and the different ways in which each of these belief systems require us to behave, generate conflict among different groups. This reality is counterintuitive and harmful and conflicts with what it really means to be spiritual and to act compassionately, honestly, and peacefully.

Fortunately, we can nurture our understanding and broaden our vision to embrace universal truth by expanding our insight and replacing harmful social and religious prejudices with a compassionate, holistic outlook that includes everyone—even animals. We can also dismiss political and philosophical ideologies that similarly reject inclusion of animals in the moral community.

As literary scholar Erica Fudge notes: 'What is at stake ultimately is our own ability to think beyond ourselves, to include within the orbit of our imaginations as well as our material existences, those beings of other species. A failure here creates the ground for the continuation of many of those practices that we would regard as cruel and paradoxical. A failure also reveals a limitation to our own capacity, something that might seem to be at odds with the absolute power that we constantly assert over animals' (2002, 22–23).

So how might we define Truth in the context of the exploitation of animals and our response to it? Inasmuch as I know from my own experience that humans have the capacity to think, suffer, feel pain, and experience emotions, I logically conclude that animals also must be equally capable, as there's fundamentally no difference psychologically, physiologically, and behaviourally between us. I reject the proposition that human wellbeing always necessitates the subjugation of animals, or that they exist on separate moral planes. In fact, I believe they're inextricably interwoven.

More specifically, the exercise of truth means recognising our own complicity in the animal industrial complex and the need to uncover the lies of those—including ourselves—who benefit from its horrors. How deeply embedded we are in its obscenities will reveal itself to us as we dig deeper and deeper into our use of animal products. But such an investigation is necessary if we're to break through the distortions to reach a more honest and nonviolent relationship with other beings.

4

The Wisdom of Compassion

The first time I was forced to think about compassion was in 1976, when Peter Roberts of Compassion In World Farming (CIWF) interviewed me for the position of campaign officer in his organisation.

'Do you have a problem with the word *compassion*?' he asked.

'No, I don't think so', I replied. 'Why?'

'Well, some men are embarrassed by the word.'

'Not me', I reassured him.

I'll talk about how I came to be interviewed at CIWF in the next chapter. Suffice to say, my answer to Peter that day was motivated more by wanting the job than understanding what compassion meant. But his question was as significant then as it is now, and I'll spend this chapter exploring its ramifications.

Sympathy, empathy, and *compassion* are siblings in a family of nouns that describe a concern for others. Each one has a different personality. (I dislike including *pity* in this lexicon as it suggests a condescending attitude based on a belief in one's own superiority.) Whereas sympathy connotes some degree of fellow-feeling, and empathy suggests that you are in some way relating to what the subject of your attention is experiencing, compassion as I see it is about *extending* one's cognitive, emotional, imaginative, and even physical sensibilities to the other being and *acting* to lessen or end that suffering. In its emphasis on moving one from a position of passive interest to engagement, compassion is for me a key value in animal rights. It is compassion's inherent ability to motivate us to do something about the affliction we're encountering that makes it so special and fundamental.

Because it calls upon us to act, compassion can be an unsettling, even revolutionary virtue. Once activated, it can leave us vulnerable to the scorn, even violence, of others, or it can inspire them to act with us. Once experienced or expressed, it has the potential to stir us to act to help others regardless of species. Compassion encourages selflessness, dissolves prejudice, prevents violence, and promotes peace, through an altruistic love that opens our eyes, hearts, and minds to the suffering of others and forces us to make positive differences in their lives. Compassion is justice in action.

In a formulation I like, Ken Jones in *The New Social Face of Buddhism* calls compassion 'the *daily face* of wisdom' (177, his italics). The phrase 'daily face' suggests to me that compassion is the way we present what we have learnt deeply about the world to it: it's how we look at reality, and how people determine how much wisdom, and of what kind, we've learnt. Jones continues: '[H]elping others is compassion in action, whereby we seek to transcend the sense of a separate, self-absorbed ego' (177).

To live without compassion, on the other hand, is not merely to be devoid of the capability to recognise oneself in another, to place oneself in that being's situation, and then act on the discomfort that that other individual is experiencing. It's to deny oneself the very possibility of the sort of change—whether personal transformation or social progress—that could fill the heart and open the mind to still *further* change. Perhaps that's why so many of us fear the demands of compassion—that if we allow ourselves to be touched by the experience of *one* animal's suffering, for instance, we'll no longer have any way of resisting *every* animal's misery: that we may not be able to go back to the person we were or life we had before, because we're no longer that person and that life no longer holds any meaning for us.

Consider Camberley Kate. She wasn't outwardly a warm personality: compassion isn't particularly interested in conventional 'niceness' or sociability. She wasn't universally liked or admired: compassion doesn't depend on generating warm and fuzzy feelings in the body politic. In fact, in her defiance of conventional public behaviour and her refusal to turn any animal away—or deny anyone the opportunity to abandon their animals with her—Kate was both confrontational and completely accepting. Her compassion didn't care whether you felt bad for the animals or embarrassed at how she looked or behaved. She wanted you to act—to help the animals who were in her care. But if you didn't, then she wasn't going to waste her time making you feel less guilty about it.

Kate's compassion was both overt and hidden. By displaying the dogs she rescued and whom she wanted you to adopt, she was almost demanding you to run the following internal monologue: *I can't believe that woman has all those dogs! She's showing off her own virtue and that makes me angry and uncomfortable. Why does she annoy me? Is it because she's forcing me to pay attention to my own selfishness? What is my responsibility to these creatures?* Kate's in-your-face relationship with animals wasn't the only way she showed compassion. Her regular donations and assistance to the poor and the sick went unnoticed. But even this quiet thoughtfulness presents a challenge to us—because it overturns our assumption that people who overtly care about animals do so at the expense of their concern for other human beings. Given that Kate was as secret about her charity towards people as she was confrontational about her charity towards animals, how are we to hold on to our much-cherished prejudices that those who love animals must hate people . . . or vice versa?

Because compassion is so much more potentially unsettling a virtue than either sympathy or empathy, we wall ourselves off from it and disconnect from our thoughts and feelings. We exploit others and tune ourselves out of the (perhaps unconscious) violence we allow to be inflicted on other animals by telling ourselves that these creatures are insentient machines, or their experience of suffering is different from ours, or that our needs trump their pain. By reasoning our way out of our culpability and in our worry that compassion might force us to change, we curtail and undermine the very thing that makes us human: our imagination. Or, as philosopher Nancy E. Snow puts it, compassion leads us to an 'imaginative dwelling', where we connect with others (Fudge, 2008, 66).

So, compassion is not necessarily comforting. It doesn't bathe you in the warm glow of believing that you're a caring, sensitive individual. In fact, it may stimulate feelings of inadequacy, powerlessness, frustration, and even anger. To see cruelty towards animals at every turn, and to know how systematically and systemically they are exploited, is to open oneself up to emotions that sit uncomfortably alongside the demand of compassion that one *continually* open oneself up to the concerns of others and seek to understand them—even if they are people who actively or passively harm animals.

As I indicated in the previous chapter, the challenge that animal advocates confront is to transform the anger we feel about animal cruelty and exploitation into action: in other words, to force ourselves to be more compassionate! Nothing is more demanding, and nothing more necessary. It's been the ongoing task of my life to take my resentments and rage and refine and distil them into focused activities on behalf of positive change—a change that not only makes existence better for the victims of abusers' heartlessness, but offers the possibility that these same abusers may alter their behaviour, and (*and this is the crucial point*) allows me, as Buddhists would say, to safeguard my heart and open it still further to the opportunities for personal and social transformation.

In that regard, the exercise and practice of compassion present us with the chance to liberate ourselves from our prejudices and connect us with those who need our help. Compassion can break down the walls separating *us* from *them*—whether that prejudice is gendered, racial, or speciesist. Hatred is the barrier we construct to stop ourselves from feeling compassion for others. Fear is the emotion that keeps that hatred in place.

As the words 'exercise' and 'practice' in the previous paragraph make clear, compassion is, like veganism itself, not so much a goal as an orientation or journey—one we learn to recommit to as much in the breach or inadequacy of our efforts to extend it as we do through living it. In our constant failure to match its dictates and in the relentless honesty with which it probes our conscious and unconscious mind and its motivations, the practice of compassion forces one to examine just how compassionate we are to *ourselves*!

I've found out in the course of my life as an animal advocate that it's all too easy to set up your own court and be the self-righteous judge and jury to dispense justice to all those who failed to meet your expectations, act as you saw fit, or follow your unspoken laws. But genuine compassion puts your own soul in the dock and cross-examines your motivations, your actions, and your self-professed virtue—without stopping. Compassion, for instance, kept on at me: I was committed to telling the truth about our treatment of animals; but was I telling the truth about myself? Was I being hard on others because it was easier than being as hard on myself? I may have claimed to feel compassion for animals, but did I feel compassionate towards my closest companion animal: myself?

Compassion finds itself excluded from the Misanthropic Bunker. The bunker mentality has no time for genuine self-examination or an honest re-evaluation of one's behaviour or attitude. Instead, the ego establishes itself as the self-appointed 'keeper of the sacred flame' of whatever ideology it believes is the one true way. You invest so much in your creed that you transform it into an idol, whereby your means of achieving a goal become more important than the end.

Because one can never be too pure, and perfection is unreachable, the Misanthropic Bunker becomes not only a place to hide away to lick one's wounds but a fortress of solitude. Protected from the vagaries and contradictions of the world, you're free to burrow into your own feelings and turn over in your mind all the ways in which civilisation—a civilisation built on the bones and flesh of countless individual animals—has let you down. Everyday pleasures become insignificant, even obscene wastes of time. *If only you'd not known,* you tell yourself, *you'd have been happily ignorant like everyone else.* And so it goes on.

As you might imagine, such compassionless veganism is pathological. Inward-looking, obsessed with his own purity, and perversely enjoying the endless victimisation that is fed by the hatred and contempt he has for his fellow human beings and their witless malice and cruelties, the resident of the Misanthropic Bunker can scream all he likes at the injustice of the world, secure in the knowledge that his particular brand of perfection will never be adulterated by those who'll never fully understand what it means to be a *real* vegan or animal advocate, because neither he nor his ideas will see the light of day. Meanwhile, the boring, everyday work essential to building an effective social movement goes undone because it doesn't lead to immediate liberation for animals. Perversely, therefore, a failure to do anything—which is always immaculate and absolute—becomes the only honoured accomplishment.

The Misanthropic Bunker mentality manifests itself in various ways:

- If only every pro-animal group exclusively promoted veganism, we'd achieve animal liberation much sooner.
- We must abolish the property status of animals before anything else.
- We should set free all the cats and dogs imprisoned in animal shelters if their only future is a cage or death by euthanasia.
- Democracy has failed and illegal direct action is the only course to take.

The bunkered worldview allows some people to behave in ways that would otherwise be seen as out of touch with reality—such as when they imply, threaten, or use violence towards things, the environment, and people, or when they denigrate others' actions for animals and question their motives.

What might it look like to let compassion into the Misanthropic Bunker? Compassion would immediately admit that it's important to recognise one's sadness, grief, and impotence. It would accept that it's OK to feel guilt and to want to be distracted momentarily from those whose suffering is far worse than any we may endure. It would also advise us to remember that we're not the first person to have undergone these difficulties or emotions and we'll not be the last. It would point out that many individuals in other progressive social movements—such as the cause to end the enslavement of other human beings, the fight for women's rights, the campaign for civil rights, and the struggle to free one's country from colonial rule—have undergone those same feelings of powerlessness at what would appear to be the intractability and ubiquity of the oppression they were fighting.

Compassion doesn't aim to show you how insignificant or mundane your experiences are, but to make you aware of your continuity and commonality with all those engaged in an effort to make our world more just. By its very nature, a social conscience is burdensome; if it were easy to bring about change, then it would already have happened. That the subjects of your concern have no voice and are powerless to bring about an alteration in their own circumstances are not reasons to isolate yourself, compassion would emphasise, but to contextualise and embed yourself all that more fully within the broader efforts to extend social justice.

Indeed, compassion would urge, by helping others (no matter how partially or inadequately), we help ourselves. This applies not only in practical ways by which we can make a difference for others, but in the positive feelings we experience when we act altruistically. The satisfaction—even joy—that I receive when I help animals empowers me to feel good about, and therefore honest with, myself. I'm provided with a little more strength to enable me to live courageously, regardless of any judgement anyone may make about me and my beliefs. We cannot truly feel compassion for others if our motivation for helping them is derived by whatever benefits we may gain first.

When I think of Camberley Kate, for instance, I'm in awe at her commitment to the homeless dogs. I'm sure there were moments when she felt besieged by the never-ending supply of strays and unwanted mutts who ended up at her door, and when she loathed her fellow human beings for their callousness, carelessness, and arrogance. Yet compassion forced her to keep going—to take in yet one more dog—and in so doing provided her with the emotional means to *continue* giving to human and animal alike up to her death, and maintain the courage to love the unwanted.

As you might imagine, once you invite compassion into the Misanthropic Bunker, you find yourself no longer retreating to it as often as you once did. Compassion doesn't halt all obstacles; you will still at times feel overwhelmed by the task of creating an honest, peaceful, and just vegan society—that impossible dream! But it does mean that you're making a contribution, by adding one more step in the endless path.

They may not smile and they may have, like Kate, a fierce temper, but the most effective animal advocates are those who are content and healthy in themselves (as I was challenged to find out), and above all, honest about their motivations. We cannot expect anyone to act compassionately towards others if we look upon them with contempt. And, even more importantly, we cannot expect anyone to change their minds and their behaviour with violence implied, threatened, or used.

KIM THE CHEF VS. KIM THE VEGELICAL

It's tempting to assume that the various truths I've noted and the awakening of compassion have a linear narrative—that the road from a state of ignorant carelessness to knowledgeable concern is straightforward, smooth, and heavily trafficked, and heads in only one direction. Although some fortunate individuals may have experienced their moral awakening in such a way, it wasn't the case for me. True, within a few weeks of becoming a vegetarian, I was telling everyone (including, as we've seen, my mother) that I'd seen the light . . . and that they should do the same. But, in reality, the differences between my unenlightened self, whom I'll call 'Kim the Chef', and 'Kim the Vegelical' weren't all that substantial. More importantly, the undercurrents beneath the surfaces of both of these identities provided me with essential lessons about the meaning of compassion.

As a way to work through the different demands of compassion, let's assume that one morning on his way to work at the chicken slaughterhouse Kim the Chef (or, more accurately perhaps, Kim the Abattoir Worker) had to cross a picket line of animal activists that included Kim the Vegelical? What would the vegelical have said to the chef? And how would they have reacted to the other? It's impossible to know, of course. But I can at least try to imagine how this intriguing scenario may have played out—given that I have, at various times and to various extents, been one or the other.

As he stood outside the plant, Kim the Vegelical would have most likely shouted such slogans as MEAT MEANS MURDER! and waved placards with blown-up photographs of chickens in cages on them as Kim the Chef and his coworkers walked past him and the other protesters. The vegelical would have tried hard to make direct eye contact with the chef and his colleagues. His body language would be aggressive in an attempt to dump as much guilt as he could onto them as they went to work. After all, Kim the Vegelical believed it was immoral to kill chickens for food and working in a chicken slaughterhouse was just plain wrong. It was his right to protest against people like the chef because they were responsible for animal exploitation. He considered it important to champion moral and legal rights for animals.

Later, the vegelical would be satisfied with the stand he'd taken on behalf of animals at the ghastly place where they were exploited. He didn't particularly care about the chef and his colleagues and their circumstances—what their life-situations were, what they thought about the protesters, or whether they might be feeling any ambivalence about their work. Someone had to speak out for animals, Kim the Vegelical would have told himself, and it was now his mission to do so—loudly and forthrightly, if necessary. He had one objective: to see an end to factory farming and animals slaughtered for food.

Kim the Chef meanwhile wouldn't have been aware that a demonstration was going to confront him that morning. He would have walked quickly past the protesters without looking at them, perhaps allowing his peripheral vision to take in as much as it could without giving any indication that he might have been curious about them. In actual fact, the protesters would have intimidated him and would have made him want to get inside the slaughterhouse as quickly as possible. Even though the abattoir wasn't a particularly safe place, it would have at least felt less threatening than confronting the protesters.

Although Kim the Chef would have hurried past the demonstrators, the protest would nonetheless have made an impression on him. He would have thought more about his job at the slaughterhouse and his role in the death of thousands of chickens. He might even have felt uncomfortable for a day. But he would have also reassured himself with the fact that he'd only be working in the slaughterhouse for a few more weeks, and thus he'd soon be able to remove himself from having to think about what his labour actually entailed. Were he to have located an internal uneasiness at what he was doing and acknowledged it to himself, he would have been very careful not to reveal any serious concern in front of his colleagues. To compensate for his own unease and to avoid appearing sentimental or easily swayed, he would have laughed off the protest and made fun of the animal advocates with his coworkers.

This fictional conflict represents in some small way the various misalignments between animal rights protesters and the general public they seek to influence. What's noticeable about the confrontation is how little the actual plight of the animals inside the abattoir concerns either Kim the Chef or Kim the Vegelical. What animates them more—indeed, what seems to preoccupy them beyond anything else—is how they appear to themselves and, equally significantly, how they appear to those with whom they associate. In fact, in spite of their proximity and the fact that the conscience of Kim the Chef might have been unwittingly stirred by Kim the Vegelical's protest, neither Kim is actually communicating with, or *seeing*, the other. What we observe is a reinforcement of a pre-existing monologue about how virtuous one is or how stupid the other sounds.

In order to change, Kim the Chef would have to wait until Amanda—whom he had a crush on and wanted to impress, not least by actually *listening* to her—could get past his braggadocio and engage him in dialogue. It would require Kim the Vegelical getting off his high horse to recognise that his mother had already become a vegetarian. In both cases, a connection had to be made in which opinions were respected and a genuine reciprocity was experienced before something could shift and progress be made.

I was only one of several students who spent the summer of 1973 working inside a chicken slaughterhouse. Because I've lost touch with all my workmates I've no idea if our shared experience impacted them in the same way that it did me. I recall them as working-class folks and wives of soldiers living nearby in the military barracks. I doubt very much they had the same freedom as I did to walk away from something they'd rather not be doing. For many, working in a slaughterhouse may have been the only employment available in that region and/or for those with few skills or little education—particularly as Britain was undergoing economic retrenchment at the time.

This situation is as true today as it was forty years ago. Slaughterhouses sometimes provide the only work options in small towns or rural areas around the United States and other parts of the world—

particularly for the poor and financially insecure, women and racial minorities among them. Annual job turnover can sometimes be higher than a hundred percent. Sectors of the U.S. animal industrial complex have broken laws by employing undocumented migrant workers, who because they fear deportation have little recourse to protesting poorly compensated labour and a dangerous working environment.

Any genuine exercise of compassion here would require not only the acknowledgement of the mistreatment of the animals but also a recognition that the workers inside—whatever their individual feelings regarding animals might be—are also being exploited by a system that dehumanises as well as kills sentient beings. Only a psychopath enjoys killing a living creature, which is why so much of what happens in a slaughterhouse is mechanised *and* compartmentalised, and why, in the end, very few people are engaged in actually killing the animal him- or herself. Such a process enables you to imagine that you aren't *personally* responsible for each chicken's death, and provides you with a patina of psychological and moral protection. I certainly felt that way during my experience at the processing plant.

Relentless in its honesty, however, genuine compassion doesn't stop at making a connection between the abuse of animals and those who have few options but to enact that abuse on our behalf. It insists that we reflect on the fact that lives are being ended in that building. For all of Kim the Chef's furtive scurrying into the slaughterhouse and his mockery of Kim the Vegelical's self-righteousness, it would patronise Kim the Chef to assume that he's too ignorant or downtrodden to think of the consequences of his actions. True, Kim the Chef had choices that the other workers may not have been able to exercise. But whatever our social and financial circumstances, we're all moral beings—*is it not after all how we like to define ourselves as humans and not animals?*—and we're all open to the possibility of change, no matter how unpromising our circumstances. Even those who, like me, never looked in the direction of the slaughter and who continued to eat chickens, knew deep down that we were complicit.

That's why I'm not going to dismiss with a condescending wave of the hand the obnoxious, banner-waving Kim the Vegelical as someone only interested in trumpeting his own moral superiority rather than actually persuading another person to change. In the same way, Camberley Kate cannot simply be characterised as a 'little old lady in tennis shoes' without the condescension rebounding on us: *What makes us so superior?* It's possible that Kim the Chef would have been convinced if Kim the Vegelical and his fellow protesters had stood in silent vigil or had quietly handed out leaflets outside the slaughterhouse. But it's also possible they would have been ignored and that the in-your-face demonstration destabilised Kim the Chef enough to make him reflect. Remember: Compassion doesn't have to be passive or even polite; compunction sometimes requires a rude awakening. Moral shocks are, by their very nature, unwelcome.

The mystery of transformation, of course, is that the traces of Kim the Chef remain in Kim the Vegelical simply because the latter was literally not possible without the former. From a perspective of forty years, it seems inconceivable to me that I would have realistically thought I could make a career in the food and restaurant industry when I was so uncomfortable with preparing or eating meat. Yet had I not wanted to work in that profession I wouldn't have found it suitable or necessary to work in a slaughterhouse; and had I not worked in the abattoir, it's possible that Kim the Chef might have been able to continue in the food and restaurant industry. It was my interest in one thing I thought would be my vocation that led to my actual calling—one that, in some way, would mean the overturning of a facet of my former interest. One of my dreams, of course, is to remove all animals and their bodily products from the menu, so that future chefs may pursue their dreams without requiring a crisis of conscience or even using the word 'vegan' to describe their entirely cruelty-free cuisine. But it necessitated a crisis of conscience to enable me to see that. The irony remains that Kim the Vegelical's hope is to create a world where Kim the Chef doesn't need to know that a Kim the Vegelical is needed.

Fortunately, for me, these changes occurred when I was still a teenager. I was single and young, with no financial commitments or personal obligations. Therefore, my transition from meat-eater to vegan animal advocate entailed little in the way of coping with familial disagreements or needing a job to maintain a household.

COMPASSION UNLOCKS THE DOOR

My search for compassion—with all its unavoidable rigours and ruthless integrity—hadn't finished with my becoming a vegan. In addition to a nascent sense of compassion for animals, and an innate commitment to fairness for all, I also felt fundamentally different in one other important respect. Everyone told me that one day I'd fall in love with a woman and marry her—and the surrounding culture reinforced the message. I understood that loving women was a significant emotion I was supposed to feel, but I couldn't relate to it. From about the age of ten, I knew I was attracted only to my own sex. But this feeling was something beyond my comprehension. It took many years to acknowledge, understand, and accept.

It's clear to me now that my early animal rights activism provided me with opportunities to express the frustration, anger, and confusion I felt about myself and my sexual orientation. I kept myself busy as a vegelical by campaigning for animal rights. I felt compassion for animals, but I didn't feel compassion for myself. Advocating for animal rights enabled me to avoid dealing with the truth about myself, while at the same time bringing structure, purpose, and meaning to my life. It's also true that I became caught in a vicious cycle of self-righteousness. I enjoyed the freedom of telling everyone about how their lifestyle caused animal suffering, and then felt sorry for myself when I found not everyone I talked to became a vegan the next minute. I now believe this attitude was a way to avoid discovering who Kim Stallwood really was, even though he was with me all the time.

It's tempting—and all too easy—to conclude glibly that my concern for animals was merely a mask or diversion for my sexual confusion. It would also be wrong. I couldn't get involved with gay and lesbian rights because I hadn't come out to myself, let alone others, and becoming engaged would mean I'd have to face my true self— something I wasn't ready to do. I perhaps could intellectually have made the connection between gay rights and animal rights, that these oppressions are linked through attempting to control and suppress individual beings' lives and needs. But it would have been a pose. So I threw myself into working for animal rights. I put off any effort to understand more about myself and my place in society, and avoided any questions as to how I could shape the world based on an authentic self that had nothing more to disclose—either to himself or the world—because he was fully open to both.

I'm not an animal advocate because I'm gay. My involvement with animal rights helped me to discover compassion for myself, which led me to discover how I can live honestly, including as a gay man. Feeling compassion for animals was a means of unlocking the door to a new way of living that was honest, peaceful, and respectful of ourselves and the complex world we inhabit.

It's an unfortunate irony I only came to realise many years later that if I'd only been more compassionate with myself then I would have been a more effective advocate for animals *and* understood animal rights more profoundly. Becoming a vegan and waving a banner angrily weren't ever going to be enough as a personal or political strategy for changing society's attitude towards nonhuman animals. My veganism had opened my eyes to the barbarism of the world—a barbarism made more savage, baffling, and distressing by the fact that virtually everyone around me not only didn't consider the killing and eating of animals to be barbarous at all, but actually a desirable aspect of a 'normal' society.

And this is ultimately the greatest legacy of compassion—one that it enacts on me every moment of every day. Compassion has the power to take the sternest of souls, saw open the puffed-up chest, and conduct open-heart surgery without anesthetic. It has the power to transform veganism from a philosophy of the foxhole and a mentality of defeat into a truthful and peaceful form of engagement with the world and oneself. Compassionate veganism can inspire others to follow a lifestyle where self-knowledge and deep concern for others are united in not only what we eat or wear, but in what we say, think, and do. That's why the thoughts we have, the words we speak, and the way we behave are as important as the food we eat and the products and services we use.

5

Fighting Factory Farming

One very cold morning in the winter of 1976–77, I heard trees scream as I set them on fire. I had abandoned my career in the hotel and restaurant trade and was working as a labourer in a commercial tree nursery, uncertain about which direction my life and my concern for animals were taking me.

The scream was like no other sound I'd heard before or have since. Perhaps it was the noise of the sap burning on that cold morning, or the release of gas from the combustion. Whatever it was, the sound was so distinctive that I was forced to ask myself whether these trees were alive and I was somehow responsible for their murder. I knew rationally that this was impossible, even absurd. Trees were living things but not sentient beings. Nevertheless, the scream shocked and haunted me. It also informed my understanding of what caring deeply about animals meant.

One argument that's been employed against the rights of animals is that there's no point in worrying about any harm we may do to animals because such concern leads to anxiety about whether plants feel pain. And what's the point in worrying about animals when plants also suffer? This argument is wrong in a number of ways, not least in the fact that those who persist in eating foods of animal origin consume far more plants than vegans do. The animals who become meat first ate vast quantities of grass, grains, and cereals. If omnivores truly cared about the welfare of plants they would be vegan, or even follow a raw-foods diet, because they would be consuming fewer plants.

But let's take the above line of thought at face value for the moment, since the reason for this chapter isn't only to talk about whether plants have sentience. In burning the wood, I wasn't involved in what is ordinarily considered a violent act. I wasn't setting it on fire to damage or destroy someone else's property or because I was a pyromaniac. I'd been told to burn the wood by my supervisor, and I didn't disobey him because I couldn't see anything wrong with the request. Moreover, although trees were different from stones in that they grew and were alive, they lacked a brain stem or a central nervous system or evidence of consciousness, such as we find in animals. Whatever noise was coming from them couldn't be expressions of agony because they lacked receptors or a sense of self by which to transmute that physical sensation into a psychological experience of pain.

With some modification, these arguments on why trees don't suffer have been used over the centuries to explain why it's OK to harm animals. *Because we don't kill the animal personally or deliberately, we're not morally responsible. We've always treated these creatures this way, and my family or culture or society doesn't think it's wrong, so why should I? These creatures don't feel pain because they're automata. They don't have a concept of mind that would transmute physical discomfort into mental torture.*

Precisely because human beings have been quick to dismiss the sentience and sapience of nonhuman animals, I don't want to dismiss out of hand the possibility that the trees might have been screaming. Instead, I prefer to examine the motivations that cause us, when we're faced with questions of morality, to avoid making decisions that inconvenience us or force us to confront unwanted realities. I welcome the fact that when I burned the trees I felt guilty, distressed, and confused; far from being evidence of a misplaced sensitivity, these emotions could have presaged a change of consciousness.

I don't know whether trees and other flora feel pain or are capable of suffering. However, my experience that day taught me that we don't have licence to despoil the environment, that we must be aware of and sensitive to the interrelationships of the natural world, and that we should be extra sure that those beings who clearly *do* suffer don't do so at our hands.

These ideas were made most trenchantly and effectively by novelist Brigid Brophy (1929–1995) at the RSPCA's Rights of Animals symposium in 1977, which I attended:

What the movement against speciesism asks, in the light of the theory of Evolution, is that the present high barrier between the human and the other animal species should be displaced and re-erected between the animal kingdom and the vegetable kingdom (though evolutionists will expect there to be a no-man's-land at the border). A millennium from now, there may be a symposium on the rights of plants. Humans may be working out techniques whereby we could, for instance, derive our food exclusively from fruits, which display as it were a biological acquiescence about falling off into the hands of grasping animals like ourselves. Plants are individuals, they are sensitive, and they certainly demonstrate an instinctual will to live—that is, they assert in instinctual terms a right to live. But their sensibility and individuality are not carried on by means of a central nervous system, and at the moment that is a place where our knowledge stops and seems to be an intellectually respectable place for our imaginations (at least in practice) to stop. (Paterson and Ryder, 1979, 66)

After spending the winter and spring of 1976–77 at the garden nursery where I had this unsettling experience with the burning trees, I volunteered with Kathleen Jannaway of the Vegan Society at an animal welfare and ecology bazaar in Camberley. At the bazaar, I met Elaine, who worked for Compassion In World Farming (CIWF). I also became acquainted with people from Animal Activists, Hunt Saboteurs Association, and Beauty Without Cruelty.

I had planned to visit France that summer with a friend, but after my trip didn't work out, I found myself back at home without a job, not knowing where my life was taking me. Wondering whether I might be able to become involved in the animal liberation movement, I called Elaine, who told me that CIWF had a vacancy for a campaign organiser. She kindly agreed to arrange for me to meet her boss, Peter Roberts (1924–2006), at CIWF's offices in Petersfield, Hampshire.

The duties of campaign organiser included assisting with tabling at such events as the bazaar I went to in Camberley, helping to produce the supporters' newsletter, answering inquiries from the public, and generally assisting Peter when he gave talks at veterinary colleges and to young farmers. At that time, CIWF was a very small organisation that rented a couple of rooms upstairs in the back of an old building on the High Street. Working there were Elaine, CIWF's first and then sole full-time employee, and Thelma and Pauline, part-time researcher and assistant respectively. Peter donated his time and expertise to CIWF. Clearly my willingness not to be worried about the word *compassion* satisfied Peter, for he hired me, and without much forethought or planning, my professional career—and vocation—in the animal movement began.

Lyndum House in Petersfield, Hampshire, where I worked for Compassion In World Farming and my career in animal rights began. *Stallwood Archive*

In the 1950s, Peter and Anna Roberts (1926–2013) owned and managed a sixty-acre farm in Hampshire with a small dairy herd of forty cattle. Growing numbers of farmers had begun replacing extensive, free-range, traditional farming with an intensive, industrial form of agriculture. Flocks of chickens were removed from outdoors and put inside battery cages for their eggs and in windowless buildings for their flesh. To produce the pale, anemic flesh of veal, calves were imprisoned in wooden crates so narrow that they couldn't even lie down and stretch their legs. Pigs were crammed into crates and stalls.

Peter and Anna prided themselves on the care they took of the animals in their charge. Peter personally took barren cows to the local abattoir and watched how they were butchered to ensure they weren't bought at market by French dealers and shipped to France for religious slaughter. (Religious slaughter for the Jewish and Muslim markets does not require pre-stunning, which renders the animals unconscious.) 'I would rather [oversee their slaughter] than feel the guilt of having just abandoned them', he said (Gold, 125). Peter and Anna saw how other farmers were switching over to factory farming and even considered broiler-chicken farming themselves. But it felt wrong: As Anna herself asked, '[D]on't the chickens have any rights?' (125).

Peter Roberts, co-founder of Compassion In World Farming. *CIWF*

In 1960, Peter and Anna read a letter in their local newspaper in support of a new broiler-chicken farm in an area of outstanding beauty. The letter claimed that only 'vegetarian housewives from suburbia' were concerned with factory farming. Peter wrote a letter to the paper in reply. 'I'm a neighbour of yours. I don't quite fit into the category of vegetarian housewife from suburbia and isn't it about time you had a little bit of compassion for the flock?' (125). Peter and Anna received many letters of support. Over time, they began to lose interest in the farm itself, which they sold, and started to work on an organisation that would become Compassion In World Farming, which was officially launched in 1967.

Peter took an enormous risk in employing me as the group's second full-time employee, as I had no prior experience producing newsletters, tabling at public events, helping to organise local groups, or investigating the live export of farmed animals to France. By way of establishing my bona fides, CIWF's member newsletter, *Ag Scene*, told the story of my life so far:

As part of CIWF's continued expansion, Kim Stallwood has recently joined the team at our Campaign Headquarters in Petersfield. He completed a 3 yr Catering Course at Westminster Technical College and it was during this time that a Summer Vacational job in a chicken factory, together with a distaste for much he witnessed in catering generally, decided him to become Vegetarian. He has more recently been in catering management in National Health Hospitals but decided to leave when it became clear that he was unable to help the patients in the way he wanted. He is now a Vegan and says: 'I enjoy the work with CIWF tremendously. It is challenging and stimulating, and I have the satisfaction of knowing that I am helping in bringing about the end of factory farming as well as violence in other aspects of agriculture. Quite apart from this campaigning work, there is the more positive re-education side which concerns alternative methods of farming and an alternative diet.'

Although I was only with CIWF for two years, the experience showed me it was possible to work at an organisation whose mission I personally embraced. Peter and Anna made me feel very welcome, as if I were a member of their family. I learnt a great deal from them, particularly from our many conversations about animal welfare, vegetarianism, spirituality, and the challenge to achieve social and political change.

Among the many things I learnt at CIWF, one lesson in particular stayed with me: the importance of combining short-term goals with long-term objectives. Peter and Anna understood intuitively the need to educate people and to introduce them to the different steps they could take towards ending factory farming and feeding protein directly to people instead of through animals. One step might involve some people committing never to buy eggs from chickens in cages or eat veal produced by calves kept in narrow crates. For others, a step might entail becoming a vegetarian or vegan. What united everyone who supported CIWF were its goals: to end factory farming and promote ways to produce food that fed people directly. The Robertses sought to avoid framing CIWF as an organisation with an exclusively vegetarian or vegan agenda that only vegetarians and vegans could support.

The key to CIWF's success was to provide anyone who shared the Robertses' concerns regarding factory farming and world hunger with a role at the organisation. The only qualification you needed was to be committed to ending factory farming and replacing it with humane, organic, and sustainable agricultural systems that were predominantly plant based. CIWF doesn't give, as some animal welfare groups do, its imprimatur to farmers who use non–factory farming methods. Nor does it lend its name, and thereby its reputation, to farmers who then signal to consumers that their non–factory farmed products are acceptable to eat. Instead, it publicly recognises the food industry when, for example, retailers work with farmers to end factory farming and replace it with free-range systems. This approach is an example of the strategy I discuss later—one that balances pragmatism with idealism.

MIND AND BODY AND POLITICS

Three events stand out from my two years at CIWF. Not only did they affect me profoundly but, in combination, they represent a model for the achievement of progressive individual and institutional change for animals.

In April 1977, CIWF and Direct Foods exhibited at separate but neighbouring stands at the Festival for Mind and Body in London, which was the first event of its kind. The festival attracted thousands of visitors by bringing together under one roof an amazing collection of individuals and organisations with a dizzying array of interests. These ranged from campaigning organisations such as CIWF to expert practitioners in yoga; from authors of books about flying saucers to healers who specialised in colours, rocks, music, meditation, and much more. The religious representation was similarly eclectic, with Buddhists, Theosophists, Spiritualists, Hari Krishnas, and Sufi dervishes in attendance—as well as people who were simply curious and unaffiliated with any religion or organisation. In the middle of the hall was a meditation centre where you sat quietly with New Age music playing in the background.

I found that people were hungry for information and wanted to learn. The CIWF exhibit included a life-size model of a veal calf in a wooden crate. Although many people were familiar with how veal was produced, the model enabled them to see for themselves how little space calves had. The veal calf and I became quite close friends and I would drive a white minivan with him and his wooden crate squeezed in the back to exhibit at various places.

CIWF's Newsletter, *Ag Scene*, featuring the Festival of Mind and Body, where we exhibited in 1977. *Stallwood Archive*

As anyone who's worked at a trade show for days knows, you can lose track of time. It's surprisingly exhausting maintaining a public face and an eagerness to communicate with others for hours at a time. The five days at the Festival for Mind and Body were like living in a New Age market and resort all rolled into one. I absorbed it all keenly because I wanted to learn as much as I could—even though (in spite of my experience with the screaming trees and an early experimentation with LSD) some of what I saw felt either too quaint, 'out there', or airy-fairy for my sensibilities. Much as in my initial reluctance to engage with animal advocacy, I tended to react to my attraction to New Age spirituality or what is less pejoratively called 'the human potential movement' with skepticism and disdain. I knew I'd need to work hard to learn how to separate the spiritual wheat from the material chaff.

Four months later, in August 1977, I shifted from five days at the dawn of the age of Aquarius to two days of talking to the animals, when Peter Roberts took me to a symposium organised by the RSPCA at Trinity College, Cambridge. This event, which was called 'The Rights of Animals', was as illuminating in its own way as the Festival for Mind and Body. I met and heard presentations from the philosophers Tom Regan and Stephen Clark, the authors Brigid Brophy and Ruth Harrison, the campaigners Clive Hollands (1929–1996) and Lord Houghton of Sowerby (1898–1996), the psychologist Richard D. Ryder, and the Reverend Andrew Linzey, an authority in Christianity and animal rights. All who spoke made a significant impact on my understanding of the subject and what form our campaigns should take. As with many conferences, the discussions among attendees away from the official programme stimulated me mentally and opened up a new world about our multifarious relations with animals.

The proceedings are collected in *Animals' Rights: A Symposium*, which I recommend as a summation of some of the thinking of that time (Paterson and Ryder, 1979). The gathering's significance as a watershed moment in the history of the modern animal advocacy movement can be ascertained by the response of the philosopher Peter Singer, whose groundbreaking *Animal Liberation* had been published in 1975. Singer didn't attend, but he noted in the preface to the anthology that all he could do was kick himself for not going (xii).

The conference concluded with attendees signing on to the resolution 'The Rights of Animals: A Declaration against Speciesism', which ran as follows:

> Inasmuch as we believe that there is ample evidence that many other species are capable of feeling, we condemn totally the infliction of suffering upon our brother animals, and the curtailment of their enjoyment, unless it be necessary for their own individual benefit. We do not accept that a difference in species alone (any more than a difference in race) can justify wanton exploitation or oppression in the name of science or sport, or for food, commercial profit or other human gain. We believe in the evolutionary and moral kinship of all animals and we declare our belief that all sentient creatures have rights to life, liberty and the quest for happiness. We call for the protection of these rights. (viii)

The Festival for Mind and Body had awakened in me a feeling that a re-ordering of our relationship with the nonhuman world might involve some kind of change in consciousness, and that there might be a variety of pathways to a transformed attitude towards other animals. It also made me acknowledge that some aspect of animal advocacy and vegetarianism required an awakening of the spirit, of a moving from the purely materialistic and mechanistic way of seeing the natural world into one that recognised its animating and organic forces.

The Rights of Animals symposium provided a similar 'Eureka' moment in that I discovered ideas, motifs, and conceptualisations of an ethic regarding animals. I cannot remember which speaker made me go 'Aha!' but I clearly recall experiencing the realisation that I was hearing something for the first time that articulated my thoughts for me. The conference showed me it was possible to sort out my muddled thinking so I was able to clarify and articulate what I really wanted to say.

Until that point, my mind was a turbulent mess of half-baked notions and outraged sentimentalities. When someone pressed me on what I thought, I would stammer that 'animals suffer and experience pain', that 'factory farming is wrong', and that 'there should be laws to stop it!' These heartfelt responses were expressed with passionate confidence. My self-righteous indignation empowered me to speak out but my lack of understanding meant my arguments were often ill-informed and undeveloped. I had to learn how to express myself in a way that withstood philosophical challenge. This encouraged me to learn more. I set out with no clear plan. I bought books when I saw them and read them when I could. I discussed ideas with like-minded activists at protests and in the pub afterwards. I attended presentations by philosophers, authors, and politicians whenever there was an opportunity.

I hadn't arrived entirely unschooled at The Rights of Animals symposium. I'd read *Animal Liberation* by Peter Singer soon after its first publication in 1975. Singer presented his views with admirable clarity:

> If a being suffers there can be no moral justification for refusing to take that suffering into consideration. No matter what the nature of the being, the principle of equality requires that its suffering be counted equally with the like suffering—insofar as rough comparisons can be made—of any other being. If a being is not capable of suffering, or of experiencing enjoyment or happiness, there is nothing to be taken into account. So the limit of sentience (using the term as a convenient if not strictly accurate shorthand for the capacity to suffer and/or experience enjoyment) is the only defensible boundary of concern for the interests of others. To mark this boundary by some other characteristic like intelligence or rationality would be to mark it in an arbitrary manner. Why not choose some other characteristic, like skin colour? (1990, 8–9)

Beyond its commitment to take the issue of animal suffering seriously within a philosophical framework, the book sent a clear message that a new wave of animal activists was sweeping to one side an earlier generation of those whose main concern had been to allow animals to continue to be exploited and killed as long as the cages were a little bigger and the death a little swifter. More significantly, animal activism would be placed within a philosophical framework that provided structure to inchoate impulses of kindness, charity, or compassion.

At the conference, Tom Regan was rehearsing the arguments that would ultimately become, in 1983, *The Case for Animal Rights*. Regan felt that Singer's argument that animals' *interests* should be accounted for in any decision regarding their treatment was too weak. Animals, he argued, had 'certain basic moral rights, including in particular the fundamental right to be treated with respect that, as possessors of inherent value, they are due as a matter of strict justice. Like us, therefore . . . they must never be treated as mere receptacles of intrinsic values (e.g., pleasure, or preference-satisfaction), and any harm that is done to them must be consistent with the recognition of their equal inherent value and their equal *prima facie* right not to be harmed' (329). Animals were 'subjects of a life', with their own individual biographies, and were therefore no more our property than other humans are objects for us to use as we wish, even if that use did not involve suffering.

Both Regan and Singer were at pains to argue that one could make claims on behalf of animals that weren't founded in emotion or sentiment. In other words, you didn't have to 'love' or even like animals to recognise—through logic and reason—that it was intrinsically wrong to harm them. In the 1980s and 1990s, ecofeminist scholars such as Marti Kheel (1948–2011), Lori Gruen, and Carol J. Adams began to contest the notion that our feelings for animals were irrelevant in making the case for why we shouldn't abuse them. They argued that a feminist ethic of care was

an alternative to the rights-based justice accounts that had dominated discussions within the academy and in social justice movements. Though many feminists saw 'care' as a necessary complement to 'justice,' the justice/care debate was often framed in binary terms, where our responsibilities and motivations were seen as a matter of justice *or* as a function of our capacities to care. Ecofeminists identify dualistic thinking (that creates inferior others and upholds certain forms of privilege as in the human/animal, man/woman, culture/nature, mind/body dualism) as one of the factors that undergirds oppression and distorts our relationships with the earth and other animals.' (Adams and Gruen, 2014)

Ecofeminism, therefore, offers an alternative philosophical and political approach to the issue of animal protection, as a 'loosely knit philosophical and practical orientation linking the concerns of women to the larger natural world. More specifically, ecofeminism examines and critiques the historical and mutually reinforcing devaluation of women and nature with a view to transforming existing forms of exploitation' (Kheel, 8).

I share the concern about limiting the range of our responses to nonhumans in formulating animal ethics, but I also think that at times the notion that (male) philosophers are immune to feeling has been caricatured. As we've seen, it was Regan's emotion at the death of his dog that compelled him to follow his intellect into formulating his case for animal rights. It's also necessary to acknowledge that, at the time these theories were being put forward, discussion about an *ethical* treatment of animals was too often framed in sexist and classist language as an emotional obsession of busybody spinsters like Camberley Kate (remember the 'suburban housewife' jibe that Peter Roberts had to confront?) and juvenile rebellion such as my own.

Singer and Regan wanted to counterbalance that view and provoke a rational debate about our instrumental use of animals. Singer wrote in *Animal Liberation* that '[t]he portrayal of those who protest against cruelty to animals as sentimental, emotional 'animal-lovers' has had the effect of excluding the entire issue of our treatment of nonhumans from serious political and moral discussion' (1990, iii). Regan himself concurred in the preface to *Case*: 'Since all who work on behalf of the interests of animals are more than a little familiar with the tired charges of being 'irrational,' 'sentimental,' 'emotional' or worse, we can give the lie to these accusations only by making a concerted effort not to indulge our emotions or parade our sentiments. And that requires making a sustained commitment to rational inquiry' (xii). The Rights of Animals symposium did precisely that.

TO PARLIAMENT WE MUST GO

One of the most significant moments for me at the Cambridge symposium occurred when Lord Houghton spoke. His presentation is as relevant today as it was in 1977:

> My message is that animal welfare, in the general and in the particular, is largely a matter for the law. This means that to Parliament we must go. Sooner or later that is where we will *have* to go. That is where laws are made and where the penalties for disobedience and the measures for enforcement are laid down. There is no complete substitute for the law. Public opinion, though invaluable and indeed essential, is not the law. Public opinion is what makes laws possible and observance widely acceptable. (Paterson and Ryder, 209, emphasis in original)

Douglas Houghton, or Lord Houghton of Sowerby as he became when he was made a life peer in 1974, was a Labour MP, 1949–74; minister for the Social Services, 1964–67; and chair of the Parliamentary Labour Party, 1967–74. In the House of Lords he took a particular interest in abortion-law reform and animal welfare. Although he was chair of the board of League Against Cruel Sports and vice president of the RSPCA, he retained an authority external to the animal welfare movement, and thus provided animal protectionists with credibility, respectability, and a degree of representation within the legislative halls of power.

In 1976, Lord Houghton had been chair of the Animal Welfare Year, which involved a number of organisations joining together to bring public attention to legislation pertaining to animals. In a statement, Animal Welfare Year defined its objective as mobilising the public to 'revise and bring up-to-date present legislation, and for the introduction of new legislation—*Where the Emphasis must be on the Protection and Wellbeing of Animals and not on Commercial Interest or Profit*' (Hollands, 158, emphasis in original).

The year 1976 had been chosen because it was the centenary of the Cruelty to Animals Act, which had regulated the use of animals in research. Animal Welfare Year had engaged many of Britain's organisations and the result had led to the formation in 1977 of GEC-CAP, or the General Election Coordinating Committee for Animal Protection. The aim was to maintain the momentum of the Animal Welfare Year to build an effective movement focused on public policy and directed towards shaping parliamentary activity by influencing not only who'd be elected to parliament but the platforms of the party those individuals represented.

To that end, Lord Houghton and Clive Hollands established joint consultative bodies to provide structure and opportunity for like-minded organisations to work together towards shared objectives. These bodies were the Christian Consultative Council for the Welfare of Animals, which consisted of six organisations; the Committee for the Reform of Animal Experimentation (four organisations); the Farm Animal Welfare Co-Ordinating Executive (thirteen); the Humane Education Council (twenty-five); and the National Joint Equine Welfare Committee (twenty organisations). GECCAP brought together representatives from each of these joint consultative bodies and from the League Against Cruel Sports as part of, as the slogan ran, PUTTING ANIMALS INTO POLITICS.

General Election Coordinating Committee for Animal Protection's
Putting Animals into Politics manifesto for the U.K. general election in 1979.
Stallwood Archive

Lord Houghton was in earnest when he told the conference that
to 'Parliament we must go.' The then Labour government held a very
slender majority in the House of Commons, propped up by the Liberal party, and an election could be called at any time before 1979,
when the government's five-year term expired. But Lord Houghton
wasn't thinking solely about elections in one or two years. His vision
encompassed many parliamentary cycles—utilising the period of a
general election, when the country was focused on deciding which
political party would form the next government and its policies, to
encourage candidates, parties, and the public to focus on issues pertaining to animal welfare.

Peter Roberts and I went to London to attend the meeting, chaired by Lord Houghton, in which GECCAP was formed. By the time of the 1979 election—GECCAP's first campaign—I had moved on from CIWF to the British Union for the Abolition of Vivisection (BUAV). That election and the later 1983 campaign that we took part in as GECCAP taught me just how vital it was to engage with the political process, and not merely to raise the consciousness of the general public or to provide public pressure from without. It made abundantly clear to me how much political power matters and how crucial legislation is. Ensuring that those who make laws hear your voice, understand and sympathise with your issue, and are supported for their decisions in your favour are essential if animals are going to receive the protections they need.

By the end of 1977, I'd been exposed to several experiences that would carry me forward over the remaining decades. In their very different ways, they revealed to me that the animal rights movement would only be successful if it utilised *and* coordinated a range of activities in mutually supportive strategies focused on shaping public opinion and enacting public policy.

Yes, it was vital to open people's hearts about other animals and allow them to reconnect with their compassion, such as I had attempted to do at the Festival for Mind and Body. The animal protection movement had, after all, received a great deal of its impetus at the end of the eighteenth century from people motivated by spirituality and the commandments of their faith, and several leaders of the animal advocacy movement at the end of the nineteenth were deeply influenced by spiritualism. Indeed, the vegetarian chef Rose Elliot was the grand-daughter of spiritualists and an astrologer herself. But a robust ethical grounding, such as had been demonstrated at The Rights of Animals symposium, was ultimately necessary in order to counteract those who might dismiss our opinions and sensibilities as mere sentimentality or woo-woo mysticism.

Likewise, a set of ethical and normative behaviours based on logic and reason and grounded in science were very important if animal advocacy was to have the weight of intellectual respectability and the data out of which public policy could be formulated. But logic and reason might not be enough to move us to act. We are not (thankfully) solely rational creatures. And neither of these worldviews would be adequate without specific laws and policies, such as Lord Houghton had articulated, that would force human beings to be punished for violating animals' welfare and abridging their rights. Such laws would not only reflect a changed consciousness and a robust ethical structure but actually encourage the development of compassion by redirecting human behaviour towards more humane practices.

I'm truly grateful for the opportunity that Peter and Anna Roberts gave me by employing me at CIWF—and it's a joy to find myself, almost forty years on, returning to CIWF as a consultant on a number of issues. However, by 1978 I was a vegelical in a hurry. I wanted to move on to new opportunities with other animal welfare organisations.

6

Transforming BUAV

Compassion In World Farming (CIWF) was young and vigorous (only a decade old when I joined), and determined to make a difference. The British Union for the Abolition of Vivisection (BUAV) on the other hand was old and overwhelmed by the challenges Frances Power Cobbe (1822–1904) had laid down in 1898, when she'd founded it. After my exposure through CIWF I was eager to get involved with an organisation that championed animal rights, and some contacts I'd made in the movement presented me with an opportunity to join BUAV. So committed was I that I joined as an office assistant, which was in effect a demotion following the work I'd been able to do at CIWF.

Two keys to understanding the history of the anti-vivisection movement are its personality and ideological clashes, which, all too often, were intertwined and which exacerbated the tension between regulation and abolition that persists to this day—not just over vivisection but regarding rights advocacy as a whole. Anna Kingsford (1846–1888) was a doctor, vegetarian and spiritualist; Cobbe was none of these, but like Kingsford was a passionate advocate for women and the poor, even though they both came from privilege. Kingsford's doctoral thesis was on the benefits of a vegetarian diet. Cobbe founded both the Victoria Street Society for the Protection of Animals from Vivisection in 1875 and the BUAV, when the former relaxed its demand for total prohibition.

As we've seen, the work of the RSPCA was essentially conservative: to end the 'brutalisation' of the poor and working class and maintain social harmony. Its parallel tradition—vegetarianism and animal advocacy as the catalysts and consequence of larger social change—continued through the work of vegetarian writers such as George Bernard Shaw (1856–1950) and Leo Tolstoy (1828–1910). One notable British campaigner was Henry Salt (1851–1939), who founded the Humanitarian League in 1891 to advocate for ethical socialism. The author of *Animals' Rights Considered in Relation to Social Progress* (1892), Salt understood animal rights as consonant with penal reform, anti–blood sports, vegetarianism, environmentalism, and pacifism. In the early 1890s, Mohandas Gandhi, then a young lawyer in London, read Salt's *A Plea for Vegetarianism* and reaffirmed his commitment to the diet of his Hindu/Jain heritage. Gandhi would in turn credit his vegetarianism with enhancing his commitment to nonviolent resistance to oppression.

The ongoing class and gender issues inherent within the struggles of the British animal advocacy movement are most vividly exemplified by the episode of the Old Brown Dog. In 1902, Lizzy Lind af Hageby (1878–1963) and Leisa Katherina Schartau (1876–1962), childhood friends from distinguished Swedish families, enrolled as students at the London School of Medicine for Women with the objective of becoming more informed about animal research. Although the school didn't use animals for teaching, it had agreements with other London colleges who did. In 1903 at the University College, London, the two women witnessed Professor William Bayliss (1860–1924) conduct an experiment on a brown dog. In their book *The Shambles of Science*, first published in 1903, they alleged the brown dog had a wound from a previous experiment; was improperly anaesthetised while his neck was cut open; was killed by an unlicensed research student by a knife into his heart; and that students laughed and joked throughout the experiment (Lind af Hageby, 1913).

The secretary of the National Anti-Vivisection Society, Stephen Coleridge (1854–1936), read out at a public meeting extracts from *The Shambles of Science* and accused Bayliss of breaking the law. Bayliss sued Coleridge for libel and won. The court awarded him £2,000 in damages. But much public attention had been brought to the plight of the Old Brown Dog. *The Daily News* raised funds to pay Coleridge's costs.

In 1906, surplus funds from the newspaper's campaign were used to erect a statue of the dog, which was placed in Latchmere recreation grounds, south London, with the support of the local Labour council. The memorial and its inscription ('Men and women of England, how long shall these things be?') outraged medical students, who protested at the site. The statue was in turn defended by local working-class residents, particularly women, some of whom were suffragists. The situation became so inflamed that in 1910 the local council, newly elected with a Conservative majority, removed the statue. A week after the removal, some three thousand anti-vivisectionists gathered in Trafalgar Square in support of the Old Brown Dog, but nothing came of it. Finally, seventy-five years later, a new statue, which included the original inscription, was erected in Battersea Park. I recall attending its unveiling, since the BUAV, along with the National Anti-Vivisection Society, had sponsored its installation.

As the story of the Old Brown Dog illustrates, the two decades immediately prior to World War I were a high point for agitation surrounding vegetarianism, anti-vivisection, and social progress in the U.K. The devastation of two world wars and the Depression of the 1930s weren't conducive for the promotion of animal welfare, perhaps because it seemed an indulgence to care about the suffering of animals when millions of people had died or been displaced or were living in poverty. The Humanitarian League ceased operations in 1920. Some of its leading proponents, however, went on to found the League Against Cruel Sports in 1924. The Vegan Society was founded in 1944, the Captive Animal Protection Society in 1957, Beauty Without Cruelty in 1959, and the Hunt Saboteurs Association in 1963.

In 1964, Ruth Harrison (1920–2000) published *Animal Machines*, which revealed the horrors of factory farming for the first time. (The most recent iteration of her work is *Farmageddon* [2014] by Philip Lymbery and Isabel Oakeshott, which is an important and timely update on the devastating impact of industrialised animal agriculture.) *Animal Machines* was followed in 1965 by the publication of a *Sunday Times* article by Brigid Brophy called 'The Rights of Animals'. Brophy's witty, intelligent, and passionate plea signalled a return to an encompassing, holistic rhetoric not heard since the days of Henry Salt. '[W]here animals are concerned,' she wrote, 'humanity seems to have switched off its morals and aesthetics—indeed, its very imagination. Goodness knows those faculties function erratically enough in our dealings with one another. But at least we recognise their faultiness' (Brophy, 1967, 15).

PROBLEMS AND SOLUTIONS

Brophy's writing and the re-contextualisation of advocacy within a philosophical and socially reformist structure presented a challenge to the established welfarist organisations. BUAV's mission statement, articulated by the formidable Cobbe, had laid out clearly what it stood for: to 'keep unalterably before its members and the public the fundamental principle of their warfare with scientific cruelty, namely, that it is a great Sin—which can only be opposed effectively when opposed absolutely, and without attempts at delusive compromises of any kind' (Hopley, 1998, 7).

In the early years of the twentieth century, BUAV was active in Parliament and with local and national demonstrations, charity shops, and petitions. Cobbe was followed as leader by Dr. Walter Hadwen (1854–1932), who was charged with manslaughter after a girl he was treating died from tonsillitis. Although Hadwen was found not guilty, the trial nevertheless critically weakened his leadership. The anti-vivisection movement had links to the campaigns against vaccination and for women's suffrage, both of which associations made the organisation vulnerable to attacks from its enemies as at once anti-science and too radical.

BUAV nonetheless continued. It published a magazine called, tellingly, *Animal Welfare*, and following World War II formed the Animal Welfare Trust, which emerged from BUAV's efforts to save greyhounds who went from the racetrack to the vivisection laboratory after they 'retired'. This campaign, hard and worthy in itself, ultimately oriented BUAV towards animal rescue and shelter-work and away from the even tougher job of ending animal research. In the 1950s, BUAV campaigned against Porton Down (an encampment near Salisbury in Wiltshire, where secret experiments on animals involving chemical and biological weapons were conducted), and in support of the dog Laika and other animals who were being sent into space. By the 1960s and 1970s, BUAV began to respond to the government's early interest in revising the 1876 Cruelty to Animals Act. BUAV handed in a petition of 300,000 signatures to the House of Commons in 1965 in support of change, but successive governments failed to act until the 1980s.

Attempts to bring together the BUAV and the National Anti-Vivisection Society, which supported incremental change, all failed, and by the time I arrived at BUAV, the offices, which the Union had inhabited for at least five decades, were looking as run-down and worn-out as the organisation itself. Ironically, they were located at the northern end of Whitehall near Trafalgar Square in London—only a few minutes walk north of the prime minister's headquarters at 10 Downing Street and the Houses of Parliament. To be so near the beating heart of Britain's body politic but so far from having any meaningful impact on public policy on animal research was incredibly frustrating—not least after the excitement of GECCAP's foundation.

In an interview included in the first edition of Peter Singer's *In Defense of Animals,* published in 1985, I recall how when I first joined BUAV it was 'appallingly archaic and Dickensian' (182), by which I meant that although on paper the membership was around four thousand individuals, it was hard to locate any active members. The head office didn't have any means, including leaflets, of promoting its ideas or the organisation, which in turn meant that BUAV did very little, if any, campaigning.

What BUAV *did* possess were sincere, dedicated, well-meaning, and caring leaders, who, in some cases, had given years, if not decades, to animal welfare and anti-vivisection campaigns from the 1950s to the 1970s. As they'd aged, however, BUAV had fallen dormant, just at the moment that a new animal advocacy movement was emerging. The scene was set for a generational conflict.

BUAV was not alone in having slipped from its role at the vanguard of animal advocacy. The RSPCA, the *grande dame* of Britain's (and the world's) animal welfare movement, had name recognition, heritage, authority, and enough financial and other resources to be a powerful force for animals. But reflecting the nineteenth-century class-based origins of animal protection in the U.K., the organisation was dominated by people from the rural districts ('shires') who supported hunting, as well as those who saw their mandate as stopping cruelty to cats and dogs but whose earnest endeavour was to avoid having an opinion on factory farming, vivisection (even on cats and dogs), and other areas of animal exploitation. In order to change this ossified institution and align the RSPCA with new understandings about animals emerging in philosophy, science, and public interest, campaigners such as Richard D. Ryder and John Bryant were encouraging activists to vote for progressive candidates to serve on the society's ruling council and to modernise the organisation. I wondered if the same strategy might work with the BUAV.

Relocating from Petersfield in the English countryside to central London allowed me to participate in the growing number of animal rights protests taking place in the nation's capital. I also began to connect more with the network of activists that seemed to be expanding every month. As I learnt more about the imprisonment and torture of animals in Britain's laboratories in the name of scientific research and consumer safety, both of which claims were highly dubious, I resolved to communicate what I knew to the broadest possible audience and inspire them to act. Frustrated with the inactivity of the BUAV and the RSPCA, in 1978 I joined Fay Funnell and Angela Walder in founding Coordinating Animal Welfare (CAW). Our mission was to 'bring together the active members of all animal rights societies and work for unity in the movement' (Garner, 1993, 52). CAW provided activists with two forums where they could share information and organise. We set up an alternating bimonthly cycle of newsletters and public meetings on Sunday afternoons in central London, and ultimately I would found the *CAW Bulletin*.

We'd begin each meeting, which regularly attracted more than two hundred people, with an 'open-microphone' session where anyone could talk about any animal welfare issue. The one rule I imposed from the chair was that if someone presented a problem they also had to offer a solution. So, for example, should an individual speak about a circus with animals coming to their town they would also offer to help organise a protest and could invite everyone present to join them. This approach not only allowed people to voice their passion and concern within a supportive atmosphere (in and of itself an important way to build group coherence and loyalty) but it ensured that meetings didn't simply devolve into group therapy or complaints about a lack of action. Asking people to locate a solution even as they voiced a problem enabled the individual who did so to recognise that everyone had a role to play and the power to bring about positive change. They didn't have to wait for somebody in a formal 'leadership' capacity to tell them what to do. They could do it themselves.

The remainder of the meeting was devoted to a special topic: for example, the first public screening of *The Animals' Film*, the groundbreaking documentary broadcast nationally on Channel 4 in 1982; the campaign to win control of BUAV; the closure of Club Row, a notorious London street market that sold dogs and cats (some allegedly stolen) to the public and reportedly to research laboratories; and presentations from guest speakers such as Clive Hollands, Richard Ryder, and Peter Singer. Some organisations set up stalls with free information and books to sell, and we even had a table serving vegan food (Hall, 1984, 268–69).

My framed copy of *The Animals' Film* poster, an outstanding example of the creative work produced by Lawrence and Beavan, the design studio I worked closely with at BUAV, PETA, and *The Animals' Agenda* magazine. *Paul Knight*

FUR ON FIRE

By this stage in my development, I'd moved on from tabling at conferences and producing newsletters to more direct engagement with the general public. Some of my first experiences were with Fay Funnell, who also lived in Camberley, and we'd often travel together for protests and meetings. One day, Fay told me that she planned to buy a fur coat in a sale and immediately thereafter walk out onto the street and burn it. For a week in July 1979, Fay slept outside Debenhams Department Store on London's Oxford Street to make sure she was first in line to buy a mink jacket, which had been drastically reduced in price in a summer sale from £795 to £79 (then equivalent to $158). Fay feared her plan might be foiled when she arrived to discover that someone else was already camped out ahead of her. She quickly ascertained that this person wasn't interested in buying the fur coat.

Fay had arranged a schedule for her friends to accompany her. I spent two nights with her and visited her every day from BUAV's offices nearby. The day of the sale arrived and, as promised, immediately after buying the fur coat, Fay took it outside, threw it into a rubbish bin, and set in on fire. I photographed Fay, appropriately dressed in black, looking disgusted as the fur coat and all it represented burned. 'One hundred and fifty minks have died to make this jacket', she said. 'As far as I am concerned, it is just a delayed cremation for the animals.'

I highlight Fay's act because it reminds me that one person, unaffiliated with any organisation, can take a stand on an issue and receive respectful coverage. It was an act of protest *and* a bearing of witness, and its uniqueness—one person expressing her conscience—gave it a singular weight it would not have had if hundreds of people had simply thrown their fur coats away. Fay's gesture had flair and theatricality; it courted a certain danger (setting something alight on the street) without posing a real threat to anyone; and it took onlookers and Fay out of their comfort zone. She was married to a pilot, had two daughters, and looked after a nice home. In other words, she was *respectable*, which only gave what she did a memorable frisson. That's probably why I remember it so vividly after all these years.

Fay Funnell burning the fur coat she had just bought in a sale from
a department store in Oxford Street, London. *Stallwood Archive*

Fay's burning of her fur coat was an isolated action—and perhaps all the more potent for being so. However, it was not a one-off act of protest. Each Saturday, Fay and I joined other anti-fur demonstrators outside Harrods, the famous department store in Knightsbridge, London, which was organised by Animal Activists. AA functioned as the companion organisation to the Hunt Saboteurs Association in setting up protests. In fact, many of the same activists were involved with both organisations. The anti-fur demonstration consisted of more than twenty of us standing outside Harrods (which we creatively named *Horrids*) holding placards and handing out leaflets in English, Japanese, French, Italian, and German. Fay and I had plenty of opportunity to network with other activists from London and the surrounding areas and to continue our conversations in the pub afterwards. We'd talk about the latest activities, exchange ideas, and hear points of view on what were seen as the conservative organisations: BUAV and RSPCA.

Animal Activists was eventually succeeded by Lynx and then Respect for Animals as the lead anti-fur campaigning organisations. Over the years, their public educational activities made a significant dent in sales. Britain's largest fur traders reported a drop in sales from £80 million in 1984 to £11 million in the first half of 1989. Harrods closed its fur department in 1990, after 140 years of business (Garner, 2004, 191). The Fur Farming (Prohibition) Act of 2000 outlawed the 'keeping of animals solely or primarily for slaughter for the value of their fur.'

Since our protests outside Harrods in the late 1970s, the numbers of fur retailers in Britain and the coats worn have noticeably declined. If you walk down the streets of the U.K. today, those wearing fur will most likely be visitors from abroad. Unfortunately, money is still to be made from vanity, and Harrods reopened its fur department some years ago to cater to a taste that by and large remains socially unacceptable in the U.K. The challenge first laid down by Animal Activists has now been picked up by the Coalition Against the Fur Trade, which regularly protests outside *Horrids*.

Looking back on the demonstrations of those years it's easy to see the glass half-empty and wonder how it can be that fur (the cruelty of which is particularly egregious and the need for which is especially superfluous) continues to be sold in the U.K. It's a reminder that even with a raised consciousness among the general public and the passing of legislation in the U.K., social progress is neither inevitable nor permanent, especially in a globalised environment with sometimes competing cultural identities. Vanity, venality, and sloth characterise human behaviour, as do compassion and justice. Although we might expect some values to be universal—i.e. that it's wrong to wear the skins of tortured animals merely for the illusion of beauty or the expression of wealth—those values are still subject to our very human tendency to claim the moral high ground no matter what we do, because *we* are 'good' while others are 'bad'.

In my optimistic moments, I see those fur protests as an example of how relatively few of us through persistence and dedication brought a once substantial industry to a halt in the U.K. One might have hoped that fur-wearing might have gone the way of bear-baiting and cock-fighting in the U.K. as taboo expressions of pleasure, not least since (in the U.K. at least) the wearing of fur is considered déclassé—the expression of those with more money than taste. But I feel confident that the industry, such as it is, won't survive the next few decades. Ironically, when it does vanish, everyone (should they choose to re-member it at all) will no doubt express amazement that anyone ever wore fur. It's in the nature of social change—and our human wish to appear as though we've always possessed a fully formed moral con-science—that we can be indifferent or hostile to those who demand we alter our attitudes or behaviour until we've embraced their ideas, at which point we no longer remember we were ever opposed to them or their cause. Being forgotten or rendered irrelevant is sometimes the price of victory.

EXERCISING DEMOCRATIC RIGHTS

In the pub after our demonstrations, I'd try to persuade my fellow ac-tivists that BUAV, for all its ineffectuality, had tremendous potential, if only they'd join it. My colleagues were sceptical, pointing out that their own volunteer-based groups were making more of an impact through their public outreach and campaigns with much less money than BUAV or the RSPCA. I made the case that BUAV and the RSPCA were organisations whose membership elected a board of directors with final and fiscal responsibility for their activities. If we joined and exercised our democratic right to elect progressive candidates to the board of directors, then BUAV and the RSPCA could begin again with new leadership. Many activists remained unconvinced, seeing it as a badge of honour *not* to be members of BUAV or the RSPCA. Some, however, did understand the potential to radicalise, as we saw it, the two organisations, and undertaking that venture was one of the reasons why Fay, Angela, and I founded CAW.

I was soon leading a double life: office assistant during the week at BUAV, and at night and on weekends planning with CAW an overthrow of my own employer. Naturally, I worked hard to keep these two worlds apart, but inevitably BUAV's leadership realised what I was up to. Because CAW's meetings were open to the public, BUAV's Old Guard had no difficulty in sending someone to check up on me and find out what was going on. I was told I'd be fired if I chaired any more meetings. So, not wanting to miss a session, I sat outside the Conway Hall in Red Lion Square in central London where the CAW meeting was taking place and Fay and Angela chaired in my absence. Periodically, people would emerge to tell me what was happening. When we nominated our candidates for the board, BUAV's leadership realised CAW was serious and sacked me. I was now free to attend CAW meetings in person. They had grown so large that we relocated them to the Great Western Hotel at Paddington Station.

I was also unemployed. Because it was no longer necessary to commute to London, I decided to move to Brighton. I rented a squalid room in a house so close to the railway station that I could hear the train announcements in the shower. I worked for the town's parks department undertaking general gardening chores. Then I became a postman. For eighteen months I lived, worked, and socialised in a neighbourhood that's now known as the North Laines.

North Laines was a distinct mix of alternative businesses. Aside from the usual newsagents, laundrettes, and other stores, North Laines also had the first Body Shop; Infinity Foods, the whole-foods cooperative that contained a shop and bakery; and Snot, a boutique specialising in punk clothes and paraphernalia displayed in metal trashcans sprayed with graffiti. Brighton also had a homely atmosphere: When you booked a table for Friday evening dinner at Saxon's, a vegetarian restaurant in nearby Kemptown, the proprietress would ask what you would like her to cook for you. I loved Brighton, which in 1979 was a town of extremes. A thriving counterculture rubbed alongside a highly visible branch of the fascist National Front (NF). I remember one Friday sleeping over Infinity's shop with my friend who worked there, the night before the NF was due to march through the neighbourhood. We were worried NF thugs might petrol-bomb Infinity to send some sort of political signal. Fortunately, Infinity was unscathed—although I'm not sure my friend and I would have been a particularly effective deterrent if the NF had decided to attack.

Meanwhile, CAW's plan had been activated. From the time I was fired from BUAV to the end of 1980, the battle for control of the organisation was fought out at membership meetings and in the courts. Because BUAV was governed by an executive committee, or board of directors, elected by its membership, the ability to exert power and control over the organisation depended upon having a majority of members at a meeting voting for a particular slate of candidates for the committee. Should our supporters elect a majority on the committee, it would be possible to re-establish BUAV as a robust campaigning organisation. Given that the Old Guard was declining in numbers, both as committee members and voters, it was only a matter of time before we, the Young Turks, took over. In late 1980, I moved back to Camberley to live with my parents in anticipation that we'd finally secure a majority of directors on the executive committee.

I was rehired in January 1981 as BUAV's campaigns officer with responsibility for its programmes. Our revolution at BUAV sent shockwaves throughout the British animal rights movement and beyond, including the United States and Australia. With a new executive committee dedicated to revitalising anti-vivisection campaigns and a staff led by the tenacious Margaret Manzoni, BUAV became the focal point for years of pent-up frustration at lost opportunities and valuable resources that had lain dormant and were now suddenly released for the creative and energised activists.

What I call the 'radicalisation' of BUAV was the overture to a new era in anti-vivisection campaigns, and more broadly with the animal advocacy movement as a whole. By 'radicalisation' I mean two things: first, the framing of the organisation's mission and policies within a vegan, animal rights perspective; secondly, the transformation of a defunct relic of the past into an energetic association that looked, acted, and represented itself to the world as it was now. It was essential that people related to an organisation because it spoke to them of issues that mattered to them at that moment, in a manner they understood, and through media that felt modern and contemporary. This wasn't simply a marketing strategy; it was a way of 'selling' animal rights as something urgent, current, and immediate.

In the case of BUAV that meant making it the first U.K. animal rights organisation with a distinctive logo. Its recognisable black, red, and white look helped to distinguish who we were and what we had to say. We embarked on the implementation of a corporate image programme for our public education materials that included flyers, posters, brochures, merchandise, and exhibitions. In employing the graphic design studio Lawrence and Beavan, I implemented with my colleagues the first professionally produced corporate identity for any animal group, a practice that is now the norm for most. (They designed the cover for this book.)

Anthony Lawrence and Hilly Beavan, who were also animal activists, taught me and my BUAV colleagues to understand that everything you do, say, or produce contributes, intentionally or otherwise, to a corporate identity that frames how the public and the rest of world views you. Until then, I'd thought naively that we only needed to make our case for the animals in a way that made sense to us. I was beginning to learn that not everyone reacts as we did when they learnt about animal exploitation. Our slogan was EVERY SIX SECONDS AN ANIMAL DIES IN A BRITISH LABORATORY, and it was prominently used in the first-ever anti-vivisection advertising campaign in the London Underground. I recall the satisfaction of standing on a station platform and watching people read our huge posters across the tracks.

We re-launched BUAV's magazine as a bimonthly campaigning newspaper, *The Liberator*. For the first time, we included reports on anti-vivisection protests not undertaken by BUAV, such as those generated by the Animal Liberation Front (ALF) and the new regional Animal Liberation Leagues (ALL). Although BUAV wasn't responsible for these organisations' civil disobedience and illegal activities, we developed a relationship with the ALF Press Office and with the various ALLs. For example, information obtained from documents taken by the South East Animal Liberation League about Mone, a ten-year-old female breeding macaque monkey held by the Royal College of Surgeons (RCS) of England at its laboratory in Downe, Kent, led to our successful prosecution of the RCS under the Protection of Animals Act of 1911. Although the conviction was subsequently overturned on a technicality, I learnt that, empowered with the right information and using the law, it was possible to hold people who use animals accountable for their actions. It's my understanding that the Animal Liberation Leagues were forerunners to the 'open rescues' pioneered by Patty Mark in Australia some years later.

The sincere but polite activities of the post–World War II period were replaced with forceful demonstrations and professionally produced campaigns. I helped develop the annual protests for World Day for Laboratory Animals, which included six national demonstrations with one involving as many as nine thousand protesters. The first of these, in 1982, involved six thousand people walking six miles from Salisbury to Porton Down, the government's warfare research laboratory. Working with Lawrence and Beavan, we came up with a brilliant image and slogan—MANUFACTURING WAR WITH ANIMALS' LIVES— which we used on leaflets, posters, and advertisements. I've always been immensely proud and fond of this image and consider it a fine example of protest art.

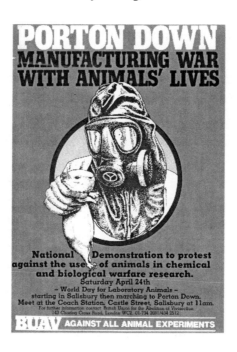

The design of this poster for a national demonstration protesting Porton Down and the slogan MANUFACTURING WAR WITH ANIMALS' LIVES, are among my favourites of the publicity materials we produced at BUAV. *Stallwood Archives*

Not only did I feel that BUAV should report on what other animal organisations were doing, but I knew we needed to collaborate with local groups throughout the country. I worked with the Borough of Islington in North London to adopt The Animals' Charter, which it did in 1983—becoming the country's first locally elected government authority to embrace animal welfare as public policy.

The charter declared, 'Animals have no votes and no representation. Animals depend on civilised human beings for protection—the protection from abuse, exploitation and cruelty imposed on them by we humans or in our name' (London Borough of Islington 1983, para 1.2). The adoption of the charter wouldn't have been possible without the tenacious leadership of Islington council's deputy leader, Valerie Veness.

In urging the creation and adoption of the charter, I aimed to place animal advocacy firmly within the reformist traditions of aspirational documents extending back to the Magna Carta of 1215, and most specifically the list of demands (the secret ballot, payment of MPs, annual parliaments, and universal male suffrage among them) called 'The People's Charter', which had been drawn up in 1838. Like 'The People's Charter', some of our demands may have struck people as too moderate, others as too radical. But the aim was to establish an idea around which people could rally and apply pressure for change—and make it clear to friend and foe alike where we stood.

We were under no illusions that this wouldn't take time. The supporters of the 1838 document, known as the Chartists, galvanised over a decade hundreds of thousands of people in campaigns that raised the issues' visibility and pressured politicians to implement many of them—sometimes as a way to lessen the chance of more radical constitutional changes, or even potential revolution. Some of their goals weren't achieved until many decades later; but at least they had been articulated.

The Animals' Charter was essential for another reason. I felt it was fundamental to involve politicians, not only because they were the people's representatives but also to show both advocates and opponents that the legislative and executive branches were *natural*, even *appropriate* venues for concern and action on behalf of animals. Having drafted the charter along with officials from Islington council, I represented the animal movement when the charter was formally presented. I was obliged to speak in front of the entire council and answer questions from its members. This, too, served an important purpose, since some of these individuals were to become in due course major national political figures, and I know we conscientised and educated a number of them on our issues. Later, they would be our advocates in the halls of power. Fifty to a hundred activists joined me in the council to urge (and celebrate) the adoption. I recall some of my fellow advocates crying because they couldn't believe such a development was possible—yet another positive outcome for our too-often beleaguered and self-sabotaging movement.

As it turned out, the most substantive direct outcome of the council's adoption of the charter was that the Borough of Islington redirected some of its pest control budget to fund low-cost spaying and neutering through the support of SNIP, the Society for Neutering Islington's Pussies! I believe this work continues to this day.

My interest in making the government responsible for the way in which society treats animals continued with GECCAP for the 1983 general election. Like the 1979 campaign, we called for a Permanent Council for Animal Protection and for action to be taken regarding the livestock trade, factory farming, experiments on living animals, wildlife, and companion animals. We ensured animal welfare remained a prominent topic during the general election, contacting the parliamentary candidates from all three major parties (Conservative, Labour, and Liberal). Along with the International Fund for Animal Welfare (IFAW) and the League Against Cruel Sports, we published material for members and supporters urging them to vote Labour, as its manifesto made the clearest and most positive commitments to animal welfare. However, the return of a Conservative government, led by Margaret Thatcher (1925–2013) with a massively increased majority, signalled that animal welfare would not be taken seriously in the new parliament.

When the Animals (Scientific Procedures) Act became law in 1986, I was the secretary for the Mobilisation for Laboratory Animals, a coalition of four national anti-vivisection organisations (BUAV, Animal Aid, the National Anti-Vivisection Society, and the Scottish Anti-Vivisection Society). We opposed this law because it wouldn't even ban particularly egregious examples of animal experimentation—such as using animals for testing the negative effects of tobacco and alcohol (!), and the toxicity of cosmetics, as well as employing animals in research for military and psychological purposes. These experiments had been the focus of the 1979 and 1983 GEC-

CAP campaigns I helped to lead. We organised a lobby of Parliament, which was attended by seven hundred people, and a rally, emceed by myself, with sympathetic Members of Parliament of all political parties, and others.

I also managed a rally in London's Trafalgar Square with nine thousand people, six hundred of whom participated in street theatre. The gathering was to that point the world's largest animal rights demonstration, with the greatest number ever involved in street theatre. Under BUAV's hallmark slogan of EVERY SIX SECONDS AN ANIMAL DIES IN A BRITISH LABORATORY, we constructed a large doorway, which was painted to represent an entrance to a vivisection laboratory. We dressed a couple of people as vivisectors, with bloodstained white coats, and stationed them by the doorway. From the plinth at the Square, we announced that for the ninety minutes of speeches and music a tape loop would play the sound of a bell chiming every six seconds. Each time the bell rang, large numbers were turned on the stage to count to six hundred while one of the vivisectors took a protester through the door, 'killed' them in front of the plinth, and laid them on the ground as dead animals. Eventually, the area was filled with 'dead animals'.

Although the government ignored our demands on the Act, I believe BUAV and its companion organisations succeeded in highlighting what needed to be done when the new legislation was enforced. For example, the U.K. government subsequently banned the testing of cosmetics on animals in 1997 and the LD_{50} oral toxicity test in 2001. In 2003, the European Union agreed to a membership-wide ban on cosmetics animal testing by 2013.

A REVOLUTION IN MOTION

From 1981 until 1986, BUAV was my life, although I also volunteered my time as an elected representative on the councils of the Vegan Society and the RSPCA. With respect to the former, a group of vegans saw what I had accomplished with BUAV and lobbied me to stand for election to the Vegan Society council. I immediately ran into conflict with Kathleen Jannaway, who opposed any attempts we made to move the organisation from the kind of wholesome 'brown rice, open-toed sandals, and hiking in the Welsh hills' identity that it had retained since I'd seen it on television a decade previously. Kathleen Jannaway resigned, which I now look on with regret, since she had contributed enormously to the Society, and had more to give.

Truth be told, however, Kathleen—like many leaders of many institutions—had 'founder's syndrome'. Even the most self-aware people who start organisations, or work in them for many years, can fall into a pattern whereby they believe that their management or leadership style is not only the best but the *only* way the organisation can be run. Because they have one-hundred-percent institutional memory and it was their charismatic leadership and brilliant innovation that took the start-up to whatever heights it scaled, founders tend to find it hard to delegate authority, develop talent (which might overshadow their own), or plan for their own obsolescence. The result can be institutional sclerosis, a failure to address systemic problems, resentment and high turnover among staff, and ultimately irrelevance when the context for that organisation's mission changes. Ultimately, founders may cause the demise of their own organisation, once age, illness, or the board have made it necessary for the founder to step down.

In the case of the Vegan Society, I helped lead efforts to modernise it, including the appointment of a new general secretary and opening an office in Oxford. Unfortunately, staffing issues bedevilled the organisation. However, before I stood down from the council, I managed to help the Society get a new logo, and upgraded the design of the quarterly magazine so it looked more like a modern, lifestyle publication.

As with the Vegan Society, I was elected to the council of the RSPCA on a progressive platform, and, once again, ran headlong into resistance from the Old Guard, which remained powerful. The dominant conservative ruling group used my criticism of the society's investments as an opportunity not only to expel me from the council but from the society itself. My expulsion in 1985 occurred when the society was in conflict over the bill that preceded the Animals (Scientific Procedures) Act. The society found itself benefiting financially from owning stock in animal research companies and simultaneously criticising them for their treatment of animals. Naturally, I protested this contradiction. In 2006, the RSPCA adopted an investment and fund-raising policy to ensure its actions were consistent with its animal welfare policies.

The struggle to gain control of BUAV proved instructive for me in several ways. It was my first experience with the unfortunate and not unusual tendency of animal advocacy organisations to care for their own employees and volunteers no better than the way in which the animals they are campaigning for are treated. Of course, I exaggerate. But it's unconscionable how often directors and senior management justify any unprofessional or inappropriate behaviour by claiming it's 'for the animals!' It's one thing to accept a low salary, long working hours, or uncomfortable physical surroundings because a substantial portion of the organisation's funds is being devoted to campaigns or caring for animals. It's another when the staff is expected to tolerate bullying, inadequate communication, and lack of professional development or training simply because the leadership has an exalted sense of its own self-importance, strategic brilliance, or maverick genius—or has run out of ideas and is burned out and jealous of newer and younger talent.

The flip-side of poor leadership is that, too often, animal advocacy groups fail to recognise the importance of a properly functioning organisation: with an open and graded pay structure, a clear line of authority, and a commitment to professionalism and the possibility of professional advancement. In other words, for an organisation to survive, it needs to be organised! It's all about structure and process. I consider this aspect of my work in animal advocacy to be as fundamental as the actual campaigns, which were longer lasting and more effective because of that solid infrastructure behind them.

I wish I could say I acted entirely nobly in the struggle for control of BUAV. But the conflict also encompassed another unattractive aspect of the movement: the conflict between, on the one side, animal rights advocates such as myself and, on the other, people who also cared about animals but didn't, I believed, deserve to run the organisation because of their weak or ineffectual campaigns and what I considered to be a lack of commitment to animal rights. I was, you'll remember, a vegelical who was blind to appreciating anyone else's contribution to helping animals, unless it was activism like mine. Truth be told, I was insufferable, tanked up on self-righteous indignation about how animals were treated. If saving animals meant being liberal with the truth, then so be it. If it entailed naming and shaming those who exploited animals, that too was OK. If I trampled on the interests of others and behaved disrespectfully towards them, the end of animal suffering justified the means. Something had to be done, went my reasoning (such as it was), and someone had to do it. And if I insulted or offended you, then so what?

There was one awful period at the BUAV when the executive committee was split down the middle. One half of the committee supported me and some other staff, while the other wanted us fired for alleged incompetence, even though I suspect the real reason was that we opposed the bill that would become the Animals (Scientific Procedures) Act, mainly because it failed to abolish any experiments on living animals. Given that the motion to dismiss us had not been recognised by half the executive committee, when one member from the other side told us we had to vacate the offices, we refused to leave. We began an occupation that lasted about three months and took it in turns to sleep in the office. We adopted the unusual step of unionising the staff, so that we could be protected from our own executive committee—well, half of them. In the end, our side won. It was one of those chapters in an organisation's history that was simultaneously exceedingly unpleasant and very necessary.

Once a revolution is set in motion, it's sometimes difficult to stop. The change we initiated at BUAV, which was funded by its significant financial resources, attracted some people whose interest in animal rights was sincere but whose experience was, in some cases, limited to all-volunteer-based local groups operating with minimal, if any, budgets. Their ideas on what form the new campaigns should take meant that unrest continued for years to come.

As the benefits of progressives managing BUAV and its coffers became widely understood, and as we began to implement our projects, others began to covet what we'd worked hard to achieve and the assets available to us. We became the focus of various clusters of activists who believed they were even more entitled to BUAV and its resources than our group, even though we'd had the original vision and tenacity to fight for them.

As you'll recall, BUAV was a membership-based organisation and its members ultimately decided what it should do. Some members who'd learnt a great deal from our own campaign to wrest control of the board decided to field their own slate of candidates to stop the public educational and political campaigns we were initiating, and reassign BUAV's funds for 'direct action' (the freeing of animals from laboratories, for instance) and their own organisations.

INFILTRATION AND SUBTERFUGE

I'm convinced that among these groups were people who weren't sincere in their motivations to help animals, but were *agents provocateurs* and police informants whose objective was to undermine, sabotage, and halt the progressive impetus for animal rights we were intent on accomplishing. I don't have any tangible proof to substantiate my claims of infiltration other than suspicions and circumstantial evidence. For instance, I made it a point to go to police stations after demonstrations I had organised to check up on anyone who may have been arrested and conclude the planning discussions I had with the officers in charge of policing the event. Could it have been entirely coincidental that, after one of the national demonstrations I organised, I witnessed several demonstrators at the local police station walk past me and go behind the public counter at which I stood? I watched them remove animal rights buttons from their jackets and strike up conversations with police officers in uniform, whom they were clearly on familiar terms with.

A series of large national demonstrations, which involved working closely with the police, that I organised in the 1980s. *Duncan Weir*

In addition to the police wanting to monitor and influence the animal rights movement, some companies also sought to halt the rise of organisations that challenged the way they used animals. Lest I be accused of paranoia, the McLibel trial in the mid-1990s, which became the longest case of its kind in British legal history, brought to light repeated use of undercover agents from the state and McDonald's (Vidal, 1997). The case, which activists Helen Steel and David Morris ultimately won in the European Court of Human Rights in 2005, centred on the production and dissemination of a pamphlet listing the environmental, human health, animal welfare, and other reasons why eating at McDonald's food was undesirable. According to Rob Evans and Paul Lewis in *Undercover: The True Story of Britain's Secret Police*, one of the writers of the pamphlet itself had been an undercover police officer (68). The infiltration of animal advocacy, environmental, and other social justice groups continues to the present day in the U.K. and the U.S. (Potter, 2011).

After the Mobilisation campaign, BUAV was, once again, plunged into a fractious internal dispute. The fallout, in part, led to my appointment in 1986 as the acting general secretary. It was a position I held briefly, as the following year I moved to the United States to become the first executive director of People for the Ethical Treatment of Animals (PETA).

I was proud of my accomplishments at BUAV, but frustrated with the persistent infighting and bureaucracy that stymied creativity in our programmes and campaigns. I looked forward to moving to the U.S. and the opportunity to help lead what was then the world's most exciting animal rights organisation. My years with CIWF and BUAV and the lessons I learnt would be useful at PETA, although I never anticipated how much there was to discover or how long I'd live in another country.

Britain pioneered the protection of animals; the RSPCA was after all the world's first animal welfare group. My U.K. experience gave me an advantage in the U.S. because I knew what needed to be done to make an organisation effective and a campaign a success. What I didn't realise by the time I returned to live in the U.K. twenty years later, was that the situation would be reversed—with the U.S. animal rights movement leading not only Britain but the rest of the world.

II

NONVIOLENCE

Scarcely a human being in the course of history has fallen to a woman's rifle; the vast majority of birds and beasts have been killed by you, not by us; it is difficult to judge what we do not share.

—VIRGINIA WOOLF, *THREE GUINEAS*

7

The PETA Turning Point

During my time at BUAV, I was building up a relationship with the animal rights movement in the United States. I first made contact with American activists when I was at Compassion In World Farming. My colleague Thelma had corresponded with Jim Mason, who with Peter Singer was writing *Animal Factories* (1980), the groundbreaking follow-up to Harrison's *Animal Machines*. Thelma and Peter Roberts provided Jim with information about European legislation and farmed animal agricultural practices. Jim and I first met at The Rights of Animals, that epochal RSPCA symposium in Cambridge in 1977, and immediately became good friends and like-minded colleagues.

We kept in touch via airmail, our correspondence critiquing American and British animal advocacy. We shared the same ideas about strategy. We agreed on the need to build a movement within the context of a progressive political, social, and economic agenda. It was an approach that I was to articulate in the January/February 1986 issue of *The Animals' Agenda*, which Jim had launched as a quarterly. *Agenda* and *CAW Bulletin* functioned as companion publications.

In the magazine, I wrote that it was 'essential that in the next ten years the animal rights movement develop a theoretical understanding of how society has to change to make animal liberation possible. Our movement must increase and refine its campaigning strategies; there must be more positive action on all fronts.' I continued:

We should model ourselves on other movements and learn from their mistakes. For example, animal rights organizations must work towards creating a national federation for animal rights—which could be internationally based—with an agreed on set of demands and program of action. We must start publishing more critical analyses of animal abuse: why it is happening, how it can be replaced, what is the power that fuels it? We must develop programs of action that are stepping stones to eradicating animal abuse and this action must always take place from the fundamental perspective of ending all animal suffering. We should acknowledge the power of the written word and direct action. We have to open our minds to see the necessary changes we must make in our personal lifestyles to veganism. Animal rights campaigners can no longer fight dogmatically on their own for no one wins who fights alone. The issue of animal rights has to be linked into human liberties and the links made between their suffering and ours. Above all, we have to understand the enormity of the task ahead of us and not be afraid. We should never lose heart as animal exploitation is inextricably interwoven into human exploitation and their liberation is our liberation.

In summer 1980, as I was moving back to Camberley from Brighton and anticipating taking over BUAV, I bought a cheap ticket through the now-defunct Laker Airlines to visit the United States. Two national vegetarian conferences were taking place that were easy for me to attend, and they seemed too good an opportunity to miss. Alex Pacheco and Ingrid Newkirk, who'd recently founded PETA, were at Newark Airport, New Jersey, to greet me.

I'd met Alex the previous year in England, when he was a volunteer for the crew of the anti-whaling vessel the *Sea Shepherd*, which under the command of Captain Paul Watson had rammed and disabled the Portuguese pirate whaling ship *Sierra* off the Iberian coast (Watson, 1996). Alex, along with most of *Sea Shepherd*'s crew, had left the ship before the incident, and he'd hitchhiked his way from Portugal to England. He looked me up in London—something made possible by the fact that, earlier that summer, I'd attended the 25th World Vegetarian Congress in Loughborough, England, where I'd met Alex Hershaft, a Washington, D.C.–based vegan activist. Alex H. had been advised by Jim Mason to contact me. Alex H. in turn had told Alex P. that if he ever got to England he should also call me. Never underestimate the importance of networking!

During Alex P.'s stay in England, I introduced him to various animal activists, including those from the Hunt Saboteurs Association, who took him out on a 'sab'. Alex asked me if I'd heard of Ingrid Newkirk in Washington, D.C. I said I hadn't. I had no idea how important a role both of them would play later in my life and in the animal advocacy movement as a whole.

In perhaps a sign of what was to come for Laker Airlines, my flight from Gatwick was delayed twelve hours. Since vegan meals on planes were then unheard of, I'd made some peanut butter sandwiches, but was obliged by the delay to eat them before I even boarded. When I arrived in Newark, hungry and tired, I was immediately assaulted by the humidity and heat of the July morning. I nearly took the next flight home! But Alex and Ingrid had graciously come to meet me, and there was no turning back now.

Soon, we were speeding down the New Jersey Turnpike to the first of the two conferences I was scheduled to attend. 'Do you have anything to eat?' I pleaded.

'Yes,' Ingrid replied, 'wait a minute.' As Alex drove, Ingrid reached behind the driver's seat and grabbed a can from the case near my feet. I hadn't noticed that next to me in the car was a case of Big Franks, which are canned vegan hot dogs. From somewhere in the front, Ingrid found an opener, opened the can, and held it out of the window as she drained the juice with the lid firmly in place so the franks didn't end up as vegan road kill. 'Here', she said, offering me a hot dog between her fingers. 'Want ketchup?' I barely had time to nod before Ingrid tossed back sachets of tomato sauce.

You may not think eating raw Big Franks straight from a can on the New Jersey Turnpike early one summer morning could represent very much. But it did. Not only did it seem free-spirited and exotic, but I saw two people who'd not only dedicated themselves to animal rights but had a certain tenacity and style. If you could package creativity, spontaneity, and adventure, well, it would have been found in that can of Big Franks we shared. I'm also fond of this memory as a reminder of how an organisation like PETA, which has now grown into a multi-million-dollar concern, was once vernacular and ad-hoc. And, yes, how at times working for animal rights could be downright fun!

The invitation to the reception held by PETA and the Vegetarian Information Service (now FARM) at George Washington University. *Stallwood Archive*

At a reception at George Washington University held by PETA and the Vegetarian Information Service, which was the forerunner to the Farm Animal Reform Movement (now called FARM), I met with

D.C.-based activists and learnt about their local activities. Outside of the conferences, I spent most of my trip with Jim Mason at his then-home in Westport, Connecticut. I accompanied him into Manhattan where he was interviewed about *Animal Factories* on NBC's popular TV morning show *Today*. We also met with the labour organiser and animal activist Henry Spira (1927–1998) at his apartment and went out for dinner, where I ate my first tofu cheesecake. This was truly a personally transformative moment, as I hadn't thought such a combination of 'tofu' and 'cheesecake' was possible, let alone eaten by me in this exciting and energetic city.

Jim and I discussed our respective movements. I was particularly interested in his thoughts on feminism and its relevance to animal rights, which I'd never considered before. As an adjunct to that conversation, we visited the vegetarian restaurant Bloodroot in nearby Bridgeport that was managed by a feminist collective. Jim encouraged me to read *Woman's Creation* by Elizabeth Fisher (1979) and *Beast and Man* by Mary Midgley (1980).

At that time, Jim was already developing the ideas and insights he included in *An Unnatural Order*, which introduced the concept of *misothery* to describe our species' hatred and contempt for other animals (1993, 163). Jim's book helped me to understand that that detestation is a kind of envy we have for their natural abilities. To compensate for our physical inadequacies, we exert power and control over them, and give ourselves licence to exploit them, simply because we can. It's a tragedy both for the animals and us that the only meaningful way we can demonstrate our relationship with them is through dominating them. Conversely, freeing ourselves from our exploitation of animals will not only liberate them from us, but help us to free ourselves from our own delusions and arrogance.

My American adventure energised and inspired me, and I couldn't wait to return with my enthusiasm and knowledge enhanced. In 1981, I visited the U.S. twice to speak at several animal rights and vegetarian conferences and to participate in further meetings and

discussions with activists. At the Action for Life conference, organised by the indefatigable Alex Hershaft, I shared a panel with Harriet
Schleifer and Constantina 'Connie' Salamone. Schleifer and Salamone
spoke about the relationship between animal rights and feminism.
This was my introduction to what became known as ecofeminism.

I wasn't alone in welcoming transatlantic contacts. Throughout
the first half of the 1980s, American and British activists moved back
and forth often between their respective countries. Ingrid and Sue
Brebner, Susan Rich, and Elizabeth Swart from PETA came to the
U.K. The *CAW Bulletin* and *The Animals' Agenda* published news and
exchanged ideas about what was happening in the U.S. and U.K. and
elsewhere in the world. After I became co-editor of BUAV's *Liberator*,
we reported the disturbing news of animal cruelty inside laboratories,
particularly from exposés produced by PETA. This was a conscious
effort on my behalf to broaden the scope of our journalism to activities conducted by other organisations—not only those in the U.K.,
but those beyond our borders. I was convinced that just as we could
no longer work in isolation as separate groups in our own countries,
so we needed to seek solidarity with, and information and strategic
knowhow from, activists and organisations in other countries.

PRESENTING THE PROBLEM WITH THE SOLUTION

I was greatly impressed with PETA's verve and fearlessness, and, in
particular, its strategy of presenting a problem and its solution *at
the same time.* The organisation graphically and shockingly showed
the issue of institutionalised animal exploitation in their innovative undercover investigations—most famously, perhaps, when Alex
Pacheco volunteered at the Institute for Behavioral Research (IBR)
in Silver Spring, Maryland, and documented the cruel treatment of
seventeen wild-born macaque monkeys from the Philippines. This
became known as the Silver Spring monkeys case, and their plight
caught the attention of the American public (Guillermo, 1993).

It was an astonishing accomplishment for an organisation's very first exposé. At this time, the animal research industry considered itself exempt from any political oversight and beyond the reach of public criticism. The research project involved impairing the monkeys' nervous system by severing the nerves in the spinal cord—a procedure called *deafferentation*—which has the effect of making it difficult if not impossible to use limbs normally and feel all the sensations, including pain. The researcher, Edward Taub, wanted to prove it was possible for severely damaged nerves to be repaired so that injured limbs could regain some function, which might have helped treat people who'd had strokes or accidents.

Alex, who was then at George Washington University studying political science and environmental studies, wanted to see for himself how animals in research laboratories were treated and what the conditions were like. He chose IBR because it was near to where he was living at the time. He recorded the cruel treatment of the monkeys and the filthy and macabre conditions of the laboratory, which included Taub's use of a monkey's skull and hand as paperweights.

After nearly four months of documenting and photographing the monkeys and the condition of the laboratory, including taking statements from experts whom they took into the facility, Alex and Ingrid showed their evidence to the Montgomery County police and convinced them to raid the laboratory and to seize the monkeys. Seventeen animal cruelty charges, one for each monkey, were filed against Taub, thereby placing animal experimentation under the scrutiny of the country's media. The plight of the Silver Spring monkeys substantiated the concerns that many of us involved with anti-vivisection campaigns had held all along. That egregious and even vindictive cruelty was taking place under the guise of scientific inquiry was confirmed again and again as PETA embarked on a series of campaigns featuring undercover footage from inside America's research laboratories.

Over Memorial Day weekend in 1984, the Animal Liberation

Front raided the University of Pennsylvania Head Injury Clinic and stole seventy hours of videotape shot by researchers while they experimented on animals. The research, which had received a grant of about $330,000 from the National Institutes of Health, was to replicate in baboons head injuries people received from, for example, car accidents. The lead researchers were Thomas Gennarelli and Thomas Langfitt. The experiments involved heavily restraining the baboons in devices that were then propelled at great speed to simulate auto accidents and cause brain damage. The researchers on camera referred to this process as 'banging'.

PETA produced a twenty-minute videotape called 'Unnecessary Fuss', which showed the research involving the baboons and their callous treatment by the researchers. The scientists were seen joking, laughing, and playing around with brain-damaged baboons. The scientists also smoked and ate while performing the experiments. NIH conducted a year-long investigation and renewed the grant for five more years. PETA organised a nonviolent sit-in at NIH headquarters in July 1985 that lasted four days. The grant was suspended pending another investigation. The university was later fined $4,000 for violations of the Animal Welfare Act. Soon after, the university said it was suspending all primate research in the Head Injury Clinic.

PETA counterposed these exposés of institutionalised animal exploitation, particularly in research laboratories, with practical steps that people could take (such as speaking out for animals and going vegan) that would make life better for animals. This straightforward approach of simultaneously presenting the problem and the solution became PETA's hallmark. Although other organisations had used different components of this strategy—the shocking video, the urge to stop exploitation, the legal prosecution, etc.—none so far to my knowledge had combined them in a comprehensive strategy.

In 1986, when I had an opportunity to revisit the United States after a five-year break, I made sure the trip included spending time with Alex and Ingrid. I wanted to assess PETA and to discover the secrets to its success. Seemingly inevitably, our discussions led to the idea of me leaving BUAV to become PETA's first executive director.

PRIDE IN PETA

I left BUAV at the end of 1986, after eight turbulent but productive years. We'd dragged BUAV kicking and screaming from post–Second World War polite and well-meaning animal welfarism to uncompromising, progressive animal rights–oriented political action. Nevertheless, it was time for me to move on and to take the lessons I had learnt in the U.K. to the U.S.

When I joined PETA in February 1987, it was struggling to grow from a Washington, D.C.–based regional organisation with national aspirations to a national organisation with international prospects. For this to happen, the corporate culture within PETA had to change from the one that evolved under its two co-founders, to one that provided it with a solid base for future growth. This was my task, and I'm honoured that I became known as 'Kim from England who transformed PETA'. Becoming PETA's first executive director was the best professional decision I ever made. The next best decision was the one I took five years later to resign.

I'm very proud of my role at PETA between 1987 and 1992. My leadership there drew from all my prior experience with the movement in the U.K. I learnt a huge amount during my half-decade, where I overhauled the managerial effectiveness and professionalism of a grassroots organisation, turning PETA into an internationally recognised force in animal advocacy, particularly in the areas of development, programming, corporate identity, finance, personnel, and administration. We had to relocate the office twice in Rockville, Maryland, because we grew so fast. PETA's annual budget increased more than 300 percent (from $3.5 million in 1987 to $10.5 million in 1991) as the number of our full-time staff rose from thirty-five to eighty-five during this same period.

I made sure that not only was the organisation's management restructured, but that there were written monthly reports, planning meetings each week, and biannual retreats. I supervised the complete reorganisation of the finances, including the creation of a new, computerised accounting system, financial reports, and twenty departmental budgets. I worked closely with the co-founders and the development director, Scott Anderson, on developing and implementing a very successful fund-raising strategy, which included social events, membership development, and high-donor programmes. This process involved direct mail, one-on-one solicitations, grant applications, the cultivation of celebrities, the Tenth Anniversary Membership Party, and Humanitarian Awards galas. The result of our efforts meant that membership in PETA increased from 200,000 in 1987 to 350,000 by 1991.

After working closely with the graphic design studio Lawrence and Beavan in transforming BUAV, I committed myself to persuading Alex and Ingrid to engage them also. Like many non-profits, PETA's image at the time I joined them was 'homegrown', to put it politely. I realised that if I was going to succeed in helping PETA become the organisation I knew it had the potential to be, I had to take all of the necessary steps to infuse its corporate culture with a professionally produced corporate identity. In my first week at PETA I asked to be given a complete set of every publication then used. This material was to mark the end of one era and the beginning of another in PETA's history.

Working closely with Lawrence and Beavan, who designed PETA's now internationally recognised lowercase 'e' logo to highlight the word 'ethical' in its name, I directed the implementation of a corporate image programme for the organisation's publications (magazine-style guides, shopping guides, flyers, posters, video covers, exhibition materials, etc.); house journal *PETA News*; and special publications (*PETA Guide to Compassionate Living, Shopping Guide for Caring Consumers, 10th Anniversary Humanitarian Awards Gala Programme*, etc.).

With Martha Powers, a copywriter and marketing specialist, I redesigned and re-launched the existing merchandise mail order pro-gramme with the *PETA Catalog for Cruelty-Free Living*, a thirty-two-page catalogue featuring Paul and Linda McCartney on the front cover. The annual gross income increased from $225,000 with a net loss of $50,000 in 1987, to $1.35 million with a net income of $240,000 by 1991.

If all of the above seems a long way from fighting over the leader-ship at BUAV or raiding laboratories at night or even eating Big Franks while tooling down the New Jersey Turnpike, then it is. Turning an ad-hoc expression of two formidable activists' passion into an inter-nationally respected organisation with worldwide name recognition is not the most glamorous or hands-on aspect of animal advocacy, but it's essential. For a business or non-profit to be effective it needs a clear chain of command, opportunities for advancement and growth, a unique identity and set of goals, and above all a healthy revenue stream and an active and growing membership. We might like to be-lieve, along with the anthropologist Margaret Mead (1901–1978), that a handful of people are the only ones who can change the world, but I don't see it as any coincidence that PETA became extraordinarily high-profile in the mid-1980s to the mid-1990s at the same time as it grew as an organisation. Because it had a robust structure, it could capitalise on the expansion that its visible and successful campaigns during this period stimulated to become that much more effective.

My job at PETA was a huge challenge that I welcomed—an excit-ing step in the journey I was making, which had started with CIWF and BUAV, in managing successful organisations and implementing groundbreaking campaigns. I met and worked with incredibly tal-ented and committed people throughout the U.S., which allowed me to visit places in America I never thought I'd see.

PROGRESS CHECKED

All of it, however, came to a crashing halt in late 1991. For reasons I've never quite fathomed, the relationship between Alex and, in particular, Ingrid and me changed. I somehow became surplus to requirements. I can't point to any behaviour or incident that either of them considered unprofessional or improper, and I was never reprimanded or given a negative evaluation regarding my work, either in writing or verbally. Nevertheless, I found myself being excluded from key decisions. Important information was withheld from me, and I was slowly shut out of the organisation. Although she never stated explicitly, Ingrid made clear to me that she wanted me to leave.

My experience with BUAV had provided me with an entire catalogue of signals that portended conflict, and after what had happened at BUAV I had no interest in getting involved in another power struggle that would almost certainly turn into something wholly negative—not least for the organisation I'd worked so hard to build up. I decided to resign, even though I had no other employment to go to. It was better for my professional pride and my emotional state simply to walk away and let Alex and Ingrid direct PETA as they saw fit.

Even in this very distressing situation, I learnt some valuable lessons. I was confirmed in my belief that there is, with rare exceptions, a natural limit to the time anyone should be involved in any organisation. I also realised that no one person is bigger than the organisation they work at, and that sometimes the bottleneck to development that you complain about can be you! Leaving PETA was simultaneously one of the easiest and hardest decisions I've ever had to make.

As it turned out, some eight years after I departed PETA, Alex himself concluded that he had no option but to leave the organisation he co-founded. He told Animal Rights Zone:

I'm often asked 'Why did you part from PETA, was it a fundamental issue and/or do you feel the actions by PETA are justified?' The short answer is: I left PETA because it had and has drifted far from its base, and because of disagreements over tactics. The longer answer is: The record will show that while I was there, my core focus was on developing high impact exposés which were very inclusive, and were typically made up of a combination of at least: undercover investigations, criminal and civil litigation, legislation and of course public education.

Alex's comments echo those he'd made earlier in *The Animals' Agenda*, when he said that there were many reasons for his departure: 'Everything from differences of opinion on the direction of the organization to wanting to branch out and take on new projects in a new way' (Church, 103–6).

Like Alex, I'd admired PETA's signature undercover investigations and the appealing vegan, cruelty-free living campaign. We also shared a concern about the tactics that PETA was taking. (Coincidentally, the only time I experienced any direct lobbying at *The Animals' Agenda* was when Ingrid asked Scott Anderson to call me because, he said, she didn't want our interview with Pacheco to be published.)

Before leaving PETA, I'd become increasingly worried about some of our actions, although I had initially been supportive of them. Every Tuesday morning, Ingrid and I met with the campaigns and media staff to review the progress of campaigns and to brainstorm ideas. We openly called ourselves 'media whores'. Our decisions on what actions to take were based on what we thought would get the most media coverage. We reasoned that PETA didn't have the same capacity as the media to place animal cruelty and exploitation in front of people. Therefore, the media would have to do our job for us.

Inexorably, we began to make decisions about actions whose *sole* purpose was to get coverage, regardless of whether it was positive or negative. In some cases, those actions were arguably incompatible with the philosophy of animal rights that I espoused. We believed that all coverage was worthwhile, even if it meant framing PETA and animal rights in a negative light, and even if it meant our ads were banned because they were too controversial. In fact, we fell in love with controversy. Outrage became our friend. We were determined to push the boundaries of reason and decency to its limits because it was, yes, all 'for the animals'.

At first, I supported one of PETA's most notorious and visible campaigns: the 'I'd rather go naked than wear fur' stunts. This protest was initially undertaken by a local U.S. group, and we copied it. As time went on, I became increasingly uncomfortable with the growing sexualisation of our actions. These concerns I kept to myself. However, over the course of a series of discussions with the feminist social theorist Carol J. Adams, I realised my commitment to feminism, as well as my political understanding of myself as a gay man, were no longer in harmony with PETA's approach.

The chasing after publicity at all costs and the fetishisation of celebrity and nudity seemed a long way from the brilliant simplicity of PETA's original two-part strategic approach of problem and solution. Surely, I started to believe, there could be other ways to further our mission to educate people about animal exploitation without doing it at the expense of someone else. The pandering for publicity at all costs brought PETA attention, certainly, but in my judgement it overwhelmed the brilliant undercover investigations that had initially made PETA's name. The clothing-optional campaigns were an eerie echo of the observation that my Domestic Science teacher had made about vegans in secondary school. For all their attention-grabbing, these stunts unnecessarily polarised sections of the population—including women and people who were older or overweight—without, as far as I could determine, making anyone more aware of the suffering of animals.

The disconnect between PETA now and then continues today. For example, PETA donates unwanted fur coats to the homeless claiming that it 'helps needy people keep warm' and 'counteracts furriers' efforts to portray fur as "upscale," "chic," or a status symbol'. Although this may seem a kind and thoughtful act, I find it deeply offensive. PETA is making the inference that the circumstances of the homeless are so exceptional that *only* they are eligible to wear fur. It's unclear under whose auspices PETA has the authority to license which members of society are eligible to wear fur and be exempt from the same moral concerns they would expect everyone else to abide by. The homeless are as capable as anyone of making decisions about how they want to live their lives. I suspect some reject fur for the same reasons that many others do.

PETA is intentionally and knowingly taking advantage of a particularly disenfranchised group of people. They know their circumstances will most likely lead them to accept any help to alleviate their impoverishment. They also know that the association of fur with homelessness will lessen fur's glamour in some people's eyes. This action is not only insensitive for economic and class reasons, it's also racist, as people of colour are disproportionally represented among the homeless in the U.S. To spin this exploitation of some of the most weak and vulnerable in society as a favour to them and a blow to the furriers is dishonest and cynical. It fails to address the violence inflicted upon the animals, the enduring circumstances of the homeless, or restore justice to either. In contrast to the singular focus on animal exploitation and the quiet dignity and self-sacrifice of Fay's dramatic protest when she set light to a fur coat in London's Oxford Street, PETA's exploitation of the homeless by dumping their unwanted fur coats on them sends a clear message that the key values inherent within animal rights are *not* truth, compassion, nonviolence, and justice.

If I'd had my way, PETA would have further developed the two-part strategy that made it so dynamic and attractive in the first place, and made me want to work for it all those years ago. I would have invested more in PETA's ability to document and publicise the problem of institutionalised animal exploitation using undercover investigations. I would have grown its ability to inspire people to engage in cruelty-free, vegan living without relying upon the gratuitous exploitation of others.

As effective and creative as PETA remains, I believe it could be even more so. It's perhaps a sign of PETA's success, and the challenges it faces as an organisation, that Mercy for Animals, The Humane Society of the United States, and Compassion Over Killing are now known for their undercover investigations, and Vegan Outreach for its 'Go Vegan' campaigns, rather than the organisation that pioneered them. Like BUAV when I arrived in the late 1970s, PETA has the task of reinventing itself to make it relevant and contemporary in an arena crowded with younger and more dynamic groups.

I'm enormously grateful for the opportunities that PETA provided me with. It changed my life professionally. PETA also altered my life personally in a wholly unforeseen way. I discovered that in addition to being an animal rights advocate, I was also an animal lover. And it was all because of a Chihuahua named Bubele.

8

The Magical Connection

I f you'd asked me in the 1970s and 1980s why I cared about animals, I would have told you that I was *against* animal exploitation
and *for* animal rights. *No sentient being, regardless of species, deserves to be treated cruelly, exploited, or killed*, I would have continued.
No one deserves to be treated with the violence we subject animals to.

I was proud of the fact that I didn't love animals. Indeed, having taken Tom Regan and Peter Singer at their philosophical word, I
would have argued vehemently that you didn't have to love animals
in order to be their advocate. Animal rights were moral and political
issues, and affection or feelings or an ethic of care had nothing to do
with either of these. In fact, to be called an 'animal lover' was, I felt,
a slur. As Peter Singer wrote in *Animal Liberation*, 'No one, except a
racist concerned to smear his opponents as "nigger-lovers," would
suggest that in order to be concerned about equality for mistreated
racial minorities you have to love those minorities, or regard them
as cute and cuddly. So, why make this assumption about people who
work for improvements in the conditions of animals?' (1990, ii)

By way of showing how the notion of 'animal lover' can cover a multitude of contradictions, Singer relates an anecdote in *Animal Liberation* about an afternoon tea to which he and his wife, Renata, were invited. The hostess heard he was planning a book about animals and had invited him to discuss the issue with other guests. One guest, as she ate a ham sandwich, asked if the Singers had any pets. 'We told her we didn't own any pets,' Singer writes. 'She looked a little surprised, and took a bite of her sandwich. Our hostess, who had now finished serving the sandwiches, joined us and took up the conversation: "But you *are* interested in animals, aren't you, Mr. Singer?"' (1990, ii, emphasis in original)

Although I wouldn't have called myself an animal lover, I nonetheless became highly emotional and angry when I thought about institutionalised animal exploitation. Singer's stated goal in *Animal Liberation* to prevent suffering and misery and oppose arbitrary discrimination and treat animals decently animated me.

The disapproval Singer felt towards the hostess and her guests— that they should claim to love animals by 'owning' pets and yet eating other animals, at the same time as they found strange those who neither lived with nor ate them—was my own: 'We simply wanted them [animals] treated as the independent sentient beings that they are, and not as a means to human ends,' writes Singer, 'as the pig whose flesh was now in our hostess's sandwiches had been treated' (1990, ii). However, these emotions were essentially directed towards an abstraction. Before I was capable of feeling compassion for animals more deeply, I had to learn how to connect with my true self compassionately and stop my vicious cycle of self-righteousness.

The catalyst was, as it so often is, an individual animal. In my case, the animal took the form of an irresistible Chihuahua with attitude, who stormed into my life in 1989. Bubele was a giant in everything but size. Although he wasn't as tiny as a teacup Chihuahua, he was still very small, as well as being larger than life!

Bubele/Boobaa. *Stallwood Archive*

Bubele became homeless in Washington, D.C., when the elderly woman who'd been his companion died. Bubele had spent his entire life with the woman and her husband, who predeceased her. Suddenly, Bubele found himself in an animal shelter. Even though PETA's mission at that time was the promotion of animal rights and not the re-homing of unwanted companion animals, something about this four-legged refugee defied doctrine. Ingrid was persuaded to take care of Bubele by a woman who'd plucked him out of the shelter to which he'd been taken. This woman was one of those indomitable personalities you meet in animal rescue—a true Camberley Kate. Like that redoubtable presence, this woman dedicated her life to convincing you to add yet one more homeless animal to your menagerie.

From the first day that Ingrid brought him to the PETA office, Bubele belied his name (which means 'sweetie pie' in Yiddish). He displayed a particular fondness for snapping at the ankles of everyone who crossed his path. He was also inclined to bark without ceasing at virtually all of humanity, except—for reasons he never revealed—at those whom he'd selected to be his friends, even though he'd known them only for a few days. One day, soon after Ingrid had begun caring for Bubele, she had to speak at an engagement out of town, and I offered to take the Chihuahua home with me.

Having evaluated a good many people at PETA, Bubele decided to adopt me. It's a decision that remains a mystery, but perhaps he felt a kinship with my own tendency to snap at people or moan without ceasing about all humanity. At the time, our home was shared with a rescued Labrador retriever named Caesar, who'd been adopted by my partner Gary before we met, as well as several cats. Bubele wouldn't consider going home with anyone else but me. What I call the Magical Connection was made: not only between Bubele and me, but I with my deeper, truer self.

'Me and Caesar'. *Stallwood Archive*

Bubele became my best friend and I took him to the office every day. We made a daunting combination and the rest of the PETA staff lived in fear of him. New personnel and interns at staff orientations were warned not to approach me when I was walking with him. People who had reason to meet me in my office had to telephone in advance. I'd wait outside my office with Bubele in my arms and we'd enter once the other person or persons had gone in and settled into their chairs. Once the discussion was over, I had to leave my office with Bubele before any visitors could. I'd stand outside my door with Bubele once more in my arms. Then, on my instruction, folks could get up and leave in safety. In fact, because he hated people arriving and leaving, and wanted everyone to remain in a constant state of being, I renamed the highly strung dog Zen Master Boobaa. Boobaa and I lived together for two years before he was killed in a car accident. Gary and I buried his body in our back garden and planted a tree upon the plot in his memory.

In the short time we had in his company, those who were honoured to be selected as Boobaa's friends saw a love of life that was so supercharged and excessive that it was almost unbearable to witness. He stormed around the office like an out-of-control toy steam-train to the sound of my hands beating on the floor. He loved travelling in the car with me. All of the passengers were instructed on how to safely enter and exit my two-seater Honda CRX. Fear always ensured compliance. First, I invited them to get comfortable in the passenger seat. 'Relax your arms down by your sides,' I said, 'but keep your knees together, pointing towards the windshield.' Then, I let Boobaa into the car from the driver's side. Immediately, he'd jump across and stand proudly on the passenger's knees, staring attentively down the road to be taken. Boobaa and I and our terrified passenger would then set off. At our destination, safety procedures required me to instruct the passenger to remain seated as Boobaa and I got out of the car. With Boobaa in my arms, we'd then open the passenger door, inviting the grateful occupant to finally exit the vehicle.

Even though Boobaa frequently bit me, he was the ideal dog for me. We were both stubborn, didn't suffer fools gladly, and went through life comfortably knowing our opinions were always correct. We routinely and playfully fought over one of his favourite biscuits whenever I gave it to him. He'd curl his upper lip distinctively when he was angry. But when we roughhoused, he made the same gesture in a parody of himself. He loved to share my coffee and would dip his head, his ears folded back, into my mug. When it was time for bed, he'd arrange his little brown body on my pillow next to my head (this didn't help my insomnia). As he slept, I'd worry if there was too much caffeine in his diet.

BEANO, PIGGY, AND HONEY

In 1991, a little while after Boobaa died, the same woman who brought him into my life reappeared. She needed help because her marriage was ending and she had to move into a temporary home. Sadly, she couldn't take all six of her rescued Chihuahua-type dogs with her. Could I help by taking at least three? I reluctantly agreed. *For two months only*, I said. I was still distraught over Boobaa's sudden passing. I wasn't ready for another dog, let alone three. My heart was still broken. But lo and behold, Annabelle ('Piggy'), Bambino ('Beano'), and Honey lived with Gary and me until they died of old age some fifteen years later.

Me and Annabelle ('Piggy') and Bambino ('Beano').
Stallwood Archive

I was devoted to this instant pack of three small dogs. They were a lot of work. They were supposed to be paper-trained, but they didn't always relieve themselves on the newspaper we laid on the floor. They didn't understand that this designated area of our home was where we wanted them to go.

We were renovating a row house in Canton (our waterfront neighbourhood in Baltimore, where we lived for eighteen years) at the time and the messes the dogs produced indoors were manageable, if not desirable. We drew the line, however, when Piggy peed in the bed. From then on, Gary and I lived with a piece of wood at the foot of the stairs, which kept the dogs on the first floor. They had the run of this floor, including the kitchen, the outdoor deck, and the small garden, where they're now buried. Our old house had a large front window and a wide ledge, which provided the perfect location for cushions for small dogs to lie on, sunbathe, sleep, and bark at the world as it went by. A pile of duvets by the front window became their bedroom.

Piggy was a Chihuahua mix with tan and dark brown fur. Like me, she liked her food. Like me, she was also inquisitive and bossy. Bambino resembled a miniature fawn, as he was a Chihuahua and whippet mix. He was a bit shy but very loving. Piggy and Beano were close friends. In fact, their deaths were only separated by two weeks. They lived to a grand age, although their health deteriorated as they grew older. Piggy had a degenerative disease of the spine. Fortunately, we had a wonderful vet. She prescribed medication and treatment that Piggy responded well to. Each time, however, Piggy became progressively weaker. Beano was more robust, although in time his kidneys began to fail.

Like Bubele and many little dogs, Piggy and Beano had attitude. They liked their walks around the neighbourhood and people always enjoyed seeing them. Ironically, they didn't get on well with other canines, and we could never take them to the dog park in Canton, which we helped to build with the local Canton Community Association (CCA). I believe in giving back to the community in which you live, which is why I founded CCA. Of all our accomplishments during my time with the association, the one that I'm most proud of is the dog park, a fenced-in area where dogs could play safely off their leashes. Gary designed it and in 2007 the City Council of Baltimore awarded each of us a Resolution in recognition of our 'outstanding leadership and commitment to the Canton community'.

Canton Community Association (CCA) Dog Park. *Gary Baverstock*

The Baltimore City Council Resolution recognising my contribution to the community. *Stallwood Archive*

The creation of the dog park provided me with the kind of head-aches that vegan animal advocates and community organisers face all the time—the sorts of problems that might make the ideologically pure run to the Misanthropic Bunker. I'd long wanted to create a dog run, but rats were a problem. As an advocate for animals, of course, I didn't want to see rats poisoned and killed, but much of the public viewed them as a health hazard.

In a profile for *The Baltimore Sun*, Linell Smith describes a public meeting of CCA that I chaired.

Kim W. Stallwood listens quietly, his expression difficult to read. As founder and president of the Canton Community Association, the soft-spoken activist has invited the rat-eradication specialist here to speak. But the topic is making his stomach churn. Stallwood is all for eliminating the trash that attracts the rats. But trashing the innocent rats? Just because people won't pick up after themselves? It's a moral dilemma that exposes his daily balancing act: On the one hand, Kim Stallwood, community activist, hopes that learning how to control rats will make life better for people in Canton. On the other, Kim Stallwood, animal advocate, is pained by any proposal that harms animals. (Smith, 2001)

The lesson I learnt was that lethal control of rats is never completely successful but that nonlethal approaches, such as removing water, food (garbage), and places for them to hide and live, do make a positive impact in reducing the population.

The third in the pack with Piggy and Beano was Honey. She was a four-pound scrap of a rescued terrier mix. I often wondered what Honey thought when she looked intensely at me. Like Boobaa, Honey adopted me and hated to be separated from me. I still don't know why I was given this honour. I was told Honey was a cruelty case. Some boys had put bubble gum and lighter fuel on her back. Thankfully, they didn't set her on fire.

Like Boobaa, Honey had a feisty spirit and was a lot of dog in a tiny body. Because her torso had no body fat, she had to wear homemade coats, often a twin set, throughout most of the year. Gary and I would make these by cutting up the sleeves of old sweatshirts, with the cuffs becoming her collars. I imagined that if Honey were a human being she'd be living on her own, getting by on gin and cigarettes, and making sure she knew everyone's business in the neighbourhood. I could see her in a modest home with many rescued cats. She was at her happiest, sitting in my arms or tucked inside my coat. When she lay against my chest, I hoped that each beat of my heart reassured her that no harm would ever visit her again.

Honey. *Stallwood Archive*

Whenever I could, I took Honey in the car to various speaking engagements, including a couple of times to Farm Sanctuary's hoedowns in Watkins Glen, New York. Honey was my ambassador and is still my conscience. I wouldn't have been able to look into her brown button eyes if I'd abandoned my commitment to seeking truth, feeling compassion, living nonviolently, and embracing justice. If I were to have done otherwise, I would surely have broken the Magical Connection. That remains true to this day.

I may not be able to read an animal's mind, but I could sense the desires of Boobaa, Piggy, Beano, and Honey. Beyond their basic needs for food and water, it was self-evident that they loved their treats, playing, going for walks, riding in the car, sitting on my lap, running on the beach, and spending weekends away in the woods. They let me know when they wanted all of these—or when they thought they *should* have them.

ALTRUISTIC LOVE

Boobaa, Honey, and I held a special affinity more real and valuable than all my material possessions combined. The connection I had with Boobaa and Honey enabled me to imagine what it could be like to be them. As with many people who truly love their companion animals, I obsessed over them. I would do anything to make sure they were happy and well. In doing so, I opened myself to the possibility of making myself happy and well.

One might hope this kind of relationship could be possible among us and other animals, including humans—that such altruistic love could be the foundation for our relations with others regardless of species, gender, and all the other ways we divide up those with whom we share the world. Too often, however, we withhold that love and parcel out our affections depending on those closest to us in terms of family or species.

The connection I felt for the animals who have shared my life with me reminds me that it can never be enough simply to attempt to establish moral and legal rights for animals, or even to rescue them or become a vegan or cruelty-free. We must expand our understanding of animal advocacy from the practical to the spiritual level of personal action.

By 'spiritual level of personal action' I'm not talking about following an orthodox religion or set of doctrines, although many traditions contain within them maxims about caring for the vulnerable and unfortunate and extending one's charity beyond one's own immediate circle (Kemmerer, 2012; Kemmerer and Nocella, 2011). Nor am I suggesting that it's necessary to believe in a supreme being or divine force, or to adopt the smorgasbord of ideas that were on display all those years ago at the Festival for Mind and Body. What I intend by the phrase is to emphasise a relationship that goes beyond the instrumental notion that each of us provides pleasure and company for the other, or even that one enjoys the complete devotion and lack of judgement that a companion animal may offer. I am, instead, suggesting a different kind of moral shock—whereby the heart is opened to the possibility of a love dedicated to another, regardless of species, that is selfless and absolute.

Far from being a vague notion of general responsibility for the welfare of another animal, the love instilled by this moral shock is an all-encompassing command that cannot be escaped. It's my firm belief that if everyone could embrace the Magical Connection, it would mean the end of animal cruelty and exploitation, human suffering, and environmental degradation.

This expression of altruistic love is not automatic. It's not romantic, self-regarding, sanctimonious, sentimental, or sugary. It requires effort, an open mind, and a generous heart. We have to work hard to feel it with those who we may not care about, or who may at times irritate, inconvenience, or infuriate us. Altruistic love cannot be pushed; the connection is only made when we let someone else become more important than ourselves. Are we willing to love those we don't know or have never seen? It seems an impossible task. Yet this is what it will take to know truth, feel compassion, live nonviolently, and embrace justice.

My adoption by Boobaa and Honey transformed the anger I felt about animal exploitation through the Magical Connection. My altruistic love for Boobaa and Honey helped me to be a little more at peace with myself and with my presence in the world. These little dogs put flesh and blood on my understanding of what animal rights meant. I now saw nothing wrong with claiming to be an 'animal lover'. As a result, Boobaa and Honey made me a better person. Their endearing personalities reminded me that when I looked at photographs of chickens in battery cages, for example, I wasn't just looking at institutionalised animal exploitation and all of its attendant violence. I saw, instead, individuals with a life history who, like Boobaa, Honey, and all of us, have complex psychological and behavioural needs as well as a desire to live happily and be well. My sense of compassion made it possible to feel what it was like to be locked up in a cage for an entire lifetime. Boobaa and Honey also led me to suspect that all animal advocates, even the ones who claim otherwise (as I once did), love animals, too.

In his essay 'We Need a Philosophy of Generosity', which I published in *The Animals' Agenda*, the art historian Steve Baker provocatively challenged animal advocates to think of the notion of 'animal lovers' in a similar vein to the above:

> Think of the way in which 'queer' recently has been boldly reclaimed and proclaimed by gay and lesbian activists, so that its effectiveness as a term of homophobic abuse has been greatly diminished. We live in a bizarre culture in which the media allow animal researchers to declare themselves 'animal lovers' in order to distance themselves from the so-called animal rights 'fanatics' who challenge their work. This is a clear example of an anthropocentric culture defending its own meanings, meanings that we must challenge and undo.

Animal advocates could reclaim the notion of 'loving animals'. He continued:

> This personal commitment and involvement is something that feminist writers have generally come far closer to appreciating than

have more conventional [sic] philosophers. It is also at the heart of our need for a philosophy that will be seen to be effective, relevant, and generous. One French feminist philosopher, Luce Irigaray, has proposed that far from being 'a formal learning, fixed and rigid, abstracted from all feeling,' an ethically responsible philosophy is better understood as an ongoing 'quest for love' (Baker, 1996, 44–45).

I agree with Baker and Irigaray. A 'quest for love'—or as I prefer to call it, the Magical Connection—goes to the heart of what animal rights means: an association not only with everyone else, regardless of species, but also with ourselves.

As difficult to summon and stringent as the Magical Connection may seem, it is, I believe, present in all of us. In fact, many people other than so-called activists experience altruistic love for animals. They share their homes and their lives with cats, dogs, and other companion animals, and for the vast majority of them one of the most difficult and emotional situations their household experiences is when a beloved animal companion dies. These poignant and distressing situations resonate with powerful emotions, such as grief, loss, and guilt (over keeping an animal alive when he is in pain, or putting her to sleep). These emotions are sometimes infused with the dynamics of the compromise and concealment of our confused and contradictory relations with animals. Carol J. Adams experienced that moment of reverse moral shock when she was forced to deal with the shooting of her beloved pony. Later that day, she felt disgust when she connected the meat on her dinner plate with her grief. 'I was thinking about one dead animal yet eating another dead animal', she wrote (Kistler, 14–15).

The gap between animal activists, who are, I believe, closeted animal lovers, and members of the general public, who are usually *seen* as animal lovers, is not as great as it would first appear. In fact, I've been disappointed that the animal rights movement hasn't been able to articulate more effectively the shared emotional bonds that advocates have for animals with those held between folks and their companion animals. It's surely a missed opportunity to awaken the consciences of those who'd never consider themselves 'activists'.

It's worth reiterating Steve Baker's point about the clever and insidious facet of the animal industrial complex that the animal rights movement and advocates in general have failed (at least rhetorically) to countermand, and in some ways may have unintentionally encouraged.

The public façade of the animal industrial complex is kind but authoritative, professional and scientific. It's the face of the expert animal welfarist who also happens to love animals personally, someone whom the public should trust to *know* how to treat animals (many may, indeed, be veterinarians). At the same time, the animal industrial complex presents to the public the face of the animal advocate hidden by a ski mask or balaclava and wearing black or combat gear—a threatening or bellicose image that, in the early days, advocates did little to dispel, caught up as we were in the outlaw romance of subversive, clandestine activities.

Employing the notion of the activist as a law-breaking enemy of scientific inquiry or human welfare, the authorities could confirm to the public that we advocates had no practical experience in professional animal welfare. Unlike them, we weren't experts and, further, we subscribed to a 'dangerous' rights-based ideology that believed that animals are more important than people. Animal advocates don't love animals, these men (and they were almost always men) in white coats could tell the public. Instead, we were politically motivated and cared only about animals' rights and not their well-being. In short, we were a threat to society, which the kindly scientists and farmers protected through their responsible use of animals to produce food and to cure disease.

Such a positioning was—and remains—a feint. *True* animal lovers, of course, don't breed their cats and dogs to sell to strangers to make money; they spay and neuter them to help stop the production and killing of surplus, unwanted litters. Animal lovers don't sell their egg-laying chickens for slaughter when they become uneconomic; they save them. The relationship that advocates have with their rescued animals is one based on altruism and either an explicit or intuitive understanding of animal ethics. Nevertheless, industries that exploit animals have successfully driven a gulf between the general public that loves animals and those who advocate for the animals themselves. That gap is unfortunately widened by some activists who act contrary to the key values of compassion, truth, nonviolence, and justice.

9

What Is Nonviolence?

At the heart of the altruistic bond or Magical Connection is a fundamental commitment to nonviolence. When I think of my relationship with Boobaa and Honey, and consider how it impacted how I felt about other creatures who are dependent on our treatment of them, I'm not only disgusted at the systemic violence of the animal industrial complex but incredulous at how this gulag has managed to portray itself as the protector and guardian of the animals it routinely tortures and eviscerates, and how simultaneously it has succeeded in characterising those who want to release their fellow animals from the cages, racks, and other instruments of affliction as dangerous, life-threatening terrorists.

Now, as I indicated earlier, the animal movement has sometimes played into the hands of the animal industrial complex by using language and actions that could be deemed violent. But I'm convinced that not only are these instances extremely rare and carried out by a tiny minority of advocates, but that some of those advocates are in fact *agents provocateurs*, either making inflammatory statements themselves or playing on the weak minds of those who are easily enamoured of momentary macho glory as opposed to the difficult work of bringing an end to the oppressive systems of animal cruelty.

I reject violence, regardless of species.

This book isn't the place to explore Just War theory or the legal and moral reasons why it might be permissible to defend oneself from attack. I simply want to concentrate on the ethical obscenity of our industrial slaughter of animals—a rate of destruction that far exceeds any acts that we humans have perpetrated on each other. The number of animals bred and killed worldwide for our consumption alone—estimated to be more than 50 billion annually—is over seven times the world's human population, which presently is slightly more than 7 billion (Williams and DeMello, 2007, 14).

If it were simply the termination of these innocent, sentient creatures then such numbers would be an atrocity. But the actual slaughter of the animals is only one aspect of a life of unremitting violence for those whom we utilise for food, our pleasure, or research. As I suggested in the Introduction, we've somehow excused ourselves from using the word 'violent' to describe the severing of pigs' tails without anaesthesia, or capturing orcas from the oceans and imprisoning them in tanks to perform tricks. Shouldn't we consider administering electric shocks to rats in a research laboratory or making dogs fight each other to be violent? And what about searing off the tips of beaks of baby chicks or anally electrocuting foxes and other captive wild animals for their fur? We wouldn't allow someone to club a baby seal on the head on the streets of New York. Why is it permissible on an ice floe in Canada? If killing whales with exploding harpoons isn't violence, what is?

INSTITUTIONALISED VIOLENCE

Day in and day out, farmers, scientists, entertainers, breeders, and others rape, torture, imprison, capture, kill, and violate animals on our behalf, and we continue about our business. And none of it's considered 'violence' because it's been institutionalised as the structure by which the powerful and dominant in a culture corral the powerless and oppressed. Institutionalised violence was normalised in slavery and in apartheid South Africa, and it remains so in the animal industrial complex.

Even though the bioindustrial-agribusiness systems are overt in that they don't deny they exist, they're covert in that they employ language and terms to deflect attention from their processes and regularise what is profoundly abnormal. They take advantage of people's ignorance and their preference to remain so. As Ken Shapiro explains, a 'combination of institutional arrangements, linguistic sleights of hand, and defensive operations ensure that animal exploitation persists in its invisibility' (162).

This is how victims of violence at the hands of the oppressors become fortunate beings looked after by their natural superiors who know what's best for them. As we've seen, the products of that exploitation are renamed and their origins hidden in euphemisms and a language that compartmentalises and deconstructs the individual until they're fragmented body parts. Ubiquitous and yet hidden, these institutions are only visible to those who experience a personally transformative moment and become capable of seeing what is hitherto invisible. From then on, these systems are unavoidable.

It's no surprise that those who speak out within a society that has heavily invested in institutionalised violence are ridiculed, alienated, and even indicted for doing so. These activists, too, are subject to the same occluding and misleading language that defines the institutionalised violence. They're violent radicals, misguided subversives, or revolutionary zealots who want to overturn the 'natural' order of things in favour of an 'unnatural' social structure. Those of us who've seen through the lies of the animal industrial complex live, as I suggested earlier, in a strange parallel world. We find it baffling that those who claim to love animals wouldn't see what we do.

Yet we were once blinded by the inverted rhetoric of the animal industrial complex. As the novelist and essayist Brigid Brophy wrote in her article 'Unlived Life—A Manifesto against Factory Farming', 'Whenever people say "we mustn't be sentimental," you can take it they are about to do something cruel. And if they add, "we must be realistic," they mean they are going to make money out of it' (Wynne-Tyson, 1985, 28).

THE DEFINITION OF NONVIOLENCE

As we've seen, the animal industrial complex has successfully twisted the meaning of violence—so that violence is kindness and kindness violence. To combat this violence, as I've suggested, requires the force of truth, what Gandhi called *satyagraha*: a commitment to exposing the lies inherent in violence by embracing nonviolence—or *ahimsa*.

Ahimsa (the *a* is the privative on the Sanskrit word *himsa*, which means 'harm') is central to the teachings of Hinduism, Buddhism, and Jainism, and was the grounding principle of Mahatma Gandhi's campaigns for Indian self-rule, and of Martin Luther King Jr.'s for civil rights in the United States. 'Nonviolence' is in some ways a weak translation for a word that has a much more positive connotation than the absence of an activity. Even words such as 'loving-kindness', 'peace-making', 'harmlessness', and 'benevolence' don't capture its depth.

Gandhi applied his conception of *ahimsa* to *satyagraha*. *Satyagraha* is a compound of two more Sanskrit words: *satya*, which means 'truth' and *agraha*, which means roughly 'eagerness' or 'force'. Gandhi, who first articulated this concept, described it like this: 'Truth (Satya) implies love and firmness (Agraha) engenders and therefore serves as a synonym for force. I thus began to call the Indian movement "Satyagraha," that is to say, the Force which is born of truth and Love or non-violence, and gave up the use of the phrase "passive resistance"' (Bondurant, 1988, 8).

In a struggle that must have seemed to those involved at the time as difficult a challenge as animal liberation appears to us today, Gandhi knew that what he was calling on his followers to do was far from 'passive'. His marches, sit-ins, protests, and other forms of demonstration didn't ask to be met with violence, yet he was well aware that violence might occur—because for oppression to exist it must deny the means whereby it would be compelled to abandon itself. In other words, oppression cannot admit nonviolence without deconstructing itself. Like King, Gandhi believed that the moral force one gains through being attacked *and not fighting back in the same way* would ultimately overwhelm anything that violent retaliation to the provocations and assaults of the oppressive forces might achieve. He also believed firmly that violence on behalf of his cause would only contribute to further violence and injury: 'Truth is the end,' he wrote, 'Love a means thereto. We know what is Love or non-violence, although we find it difficult to follow the law of Love. But as for truth we know only a fraction of it. Perfect knowledge of truth is difficult of attainment for man even like the perfect practice of non-violence' (Bondurant, 1988, 25).

In her insightful analysis of Gandhian nonviolent strategy, *Conquest of Violence: The Gandhian Philosophy of Conflict*, the political scientist Joan V. Bondurant describes what 'force', 'violence', 'injury', and 'nonviolence' mean within the Gandhian context. '*Force* I take to mean the exercise of physical or intangible power or influence to effect change. *Violence* is the wilful application of force in such a way that it is intentionally injurious to the person or group against whom it is applied. *Injury* is understood to include psychological as well as physical harm. *Non-violence* when used in connection with Satyagraha means the exercise of power or influence to effect change without injury to the opponent' (Bondurant, 1988, 9, italics in original).

Gandhi asked us to treat the 'how' (means or strategies) and the 'why' (ends or objectives) as equally significant. He wanted everyone to understand that they were personally empowered with moral agency to deliver self-rule for India. 'Courage, endurance, fearlessness, and above all self-sacrifice are the qualities required of our leaders', Gandhi said (Bondurant, 1988, 171). Note how all these virtues lead not to megalomania, but to a kind of servant-leadership—a way of giving people the courage and force of will to move forward together in solidarity towards a shared goal. If everyone is both a follower and a leader then no movement can be divided: each part reinforces the whole. This was my philosophy when chairing CAW meetings in the late 1970s.

Gandhi called his autobiography *The Story of My Experiments with Truth* (2007). I like the association of truth with experimentation. It reminds me that we are finite human beings wholly incapable of understanding the universe and, therefore, what Truth truly means—we are all, remember, simply birds on our particular branches of a great oak. It's in the context of our limited vision and our unique power to work with others of similar conviction to bring about positive change that we must become the change we want to see. 'We but mirror the world', said Gandhi. 'All the tendencies present in the outer world are to be found in the world of our body. If we could change ourselves, the tendencies in the world would also change. As a man changes his own nature, so does the attitude of the world change towards him. This is the divine mystery supreme. A wonderful thing it is and the source of our happiness. We need not wait to see what others do' (Gandhi, 1999).

THE CHALLENGE FOR ANIMAL ADVOCACY

Although Gandhi was himself famously a vegetarian, and Martin Luther King's wife, Coretta, and one of his sons, Dexter, adopted a vegan diet, the animal movement as a whole has, in my opinion, yet to fully embrace the Gandhian model of balancing the 'why' and the 'how' of its activism. Not only has this failure meant that our noble goals haven't been reached, but we've frequently left the public alienated and confused. We've been particularly inept at responding to the charges levelled by our opponents that we're violent extremists, incapable of dealing with *agents provocateurs*, hucksters, and bloviators within the movement who've advocated unwise policies for ill-conceived goals with indefinable outcomes.

Too often we've been sidetracked from the issue of how we might further the cause of animal rights and ensure real practical and political improvements in the lives of the animals by bitter infighting about purity of intention and lifestyle—symptoms, as I've argued, of too much time in the Misanthropic Bunker. We've found ourselves defending the tiny number of individuals who threaten violence and the vanishingly tiny number who actually employ it.

I used to be one of the defenders. I supported violence against property: for instance, smashing up a laboratory that experimented on animals or destroying a vivisector's research notes. As some individuals and organisations do today, I drew a distinction between harming any living being (human or animal) and breaking inanimate objects. At times, I'd finesse my response to certain actions by stating that while I may not have supported the violence, I nonetheless understood why it took place—even though neither my organisation nor I had any role in coordinating it. I call this the 'neither condemn nor condone' defence.

As I say, I used to hold such a viewpoint. I don't anymore.

I'm not naive: in any movement for change—no matter how grounded in the principles of *ahimsa* and *satyagraha* it may be— things are going to get broken and tempers are going to flare and agents of the state or the status quo are going to interrupt, subvert, and do all they can to fragment that movement. I'm well aware that an obvious distinction exists between harming a person and breaking a computer monitor. My objection to the activities that I formerly supported lies entirely in the *intention* behind the violence and the *strategy* (or lack thereof) accompanying it. Even if the activists don't state explicitly that their goal is to intimidate, by vicariously taking out their aggression on inanimate objects, they signal very clearly their belligerence and aim to scare the individuals who use them. After all, they wouldn't feel the need to destroy property if they didn't think it would make someone *feel* as if they'd been attacked.

Some might claim that the intention isn't to threaten but simply to stymie the continuing torture of animals, and to make the business of animal research even more expensive than it already is. Fair enough, I'd respond, but that's absolutely not how the spokespeople from the animal industrial complex, with its vastly superior resources and the sympathetic ear of the media, spin such supposedly principled demolition. They use each break-in or vandalism as a propaganda tool to tarnish all advocates as vicious sociopaths intent on ending scientific inquiry, wasting valuable taxpayer money, and threatening bodily harm to innocent researchers simply going about their business saving human lives.

I'd go further and argue that there's no difference between violence—implied, threatened, or used—against individuals or things, including property. An abusive spouse can terrorise his family by threatening to hit or harm his partner, children, or the animals in the home, even though he only lifts his hand to strike. More disturbingly, that threat may turn actual, even deadly, if the abuser feels he's not being obeyed. In some instances, abusers have threatened, harmed, and killed the family companion animal to demonstrate what they might also do to the spouse, children, and other companion animals if they're not compliant.

My concern is that incidents of intimidation—such as protests taking place outside the homes of researchers, arson, planting firebombs, making anonymous threats over the phone, as well as damaging property—not only lack a *strategic* goal but that they actually work against further animal liberation. They're also potentially the beginning of a slippery slope that may result in the very thing that animal liberation has been all about avoiding—violence towards animals, in this case human ones. (To my knowledge, animal liberationists have never killed or injured anyone in these actions.) Most fundamentally of all, however, the use of violence and threats echoes eerily the same *mindset* of exploitation, humiliation, and depersonalisation that defines the animal industrial complex.

Gandhi understood that you cannot defeat a powerful institution using its same way of thinking. You need to expose the inherent contradictions between its actions and behaviours and its stated goals and beliefs. If this requires breaking the law or bucking convention, then so be it. But as King and Gandhi realised, defiance of legal or social norms necessitates an absolute commitment to nonviolence.

In order to succeed as animal advocates, we can never allow ourselves to become and act like animal abusers and the animal industrial complex. Their reliance on violence as the norm is no excuse for advocates to behave violently. We cannot condone abuse of animal abusers if we condemn that abuse when it's directed towards another group (for instance, when the Westboro Baptist Church of Topeka, Kansas, protests at funerals and other occasions waving such signs as 'God Hates Fags' and 'AIDS Cures Fags'). There can be no double standards. The integrity of our campaign for moral and legal rights for animals lies not only in our argument, but also in how we make our case. The how and the why are one and the same. We cannot work for the rights of one while disrespecting those of another.

This is why nonviolence is one of the four key values of animal rights. It's true that war, riot, sabotage, and other forms of violent action have brought changes within a society, but they have also invariably led to more bloodshed, which has usually involved the most powerless suffering more while the powerful and their interests are either protected or reinstated. Violence doesn't create new and *positive* attitudes; instead, it retrenches and embeds repression and the institutions that benefited from it.

I don't believe for a minute that people would continue to live as vegans if their motivation was based on an animal rights movement that lied or in some way sanctioned violence or hostile attitudes to others. Once the shock tripped by the outrageous action wore off, disenchantment and resistance would set in. Perhaps this is why some vegetarians and vegans revert to eating meat, eggs, and dairy.

ANOTHER WAY

In this chapter, I've argued for an expansive vision of nonviolence that includes not only the implication or threat of using force to impose one's wishes on another, but any destruction of property or disregard of someone's moral and legal rights. I've suggested that the language and behaviour of the bully have no place in animal advocacy, and those who resort to such are not only doing our cause a huge strategic disservice, but in fact are casting a moral stain on our movement, and profoundly misunderstanding the vision of the world that the vast majority of us want—one free from human violence against other living creatures, including our own species. That said, just as I continue to retreat to the Misanthropic Bunker to rant against the indifference and cruelty of the world, so I recognise how attractive the idea of righteous vengeance against those who harm animals might appear. As I confessed, I once supported the break-ins, the liberations, and the destruction of property—even though I was never a fan of mindless vandalism or anything that put any living being at risk of harm. Thankfully, there is another way.

Since the dawn of the century, a new form of animal activism has emerged that, for me, represents *ahimsa* and *satyagraha* in action, while also responding directly to the animal industrial complex and the needs of the creatures confined in it. We signalled this change at *Agenda* with a cover feature in 1998 by Freeman Wicklund called 'Direct Action: Progress, Peril or Both?' Wicklund evaluated the effectiveness of direct action for animals and concluded with the following rallying cry and a question:

Given the animal rights movement's ultimate objective of achieving a cooperative and respectful society that voluntarily avoids animal exploitation, we should seriously consider adopting Gandhian direct action to gain the psychological force needed to rouse the public. Certainly ALF [Animal Liberation Front] direct action has rescued thousands of animals, closed abusive establishments, exposed animal exploitation, and generated much media coverage. But are we sacrificing long-term liberation on the altar of short-term gains? (Wicklund, 1998, 27)

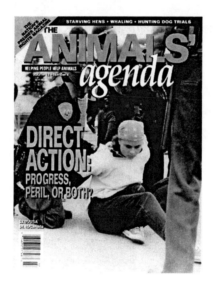

Freeman Wicklund's cover feature on direct action in
The Animals' Agenda, provoking a healthy debate about strategy in
the animal rights movement. *ASI*

We had clearly touched a nerve. The response from readers to the article was polarised. In what appeared to be an organised e-mail and letter-writing campaign, some interpreted the article as an attack on the ALF. Many demanded that the cover feature of the next issue focus on the ALF. Instead, I published two pages of letters and included as a cover feature in a subsequent issue an interview with Rod Coronado, who had completed a five-year prison sentence for ALF actions.

Wicklund's article also inspired Karen Davis, the president of United Poultry Concerns (UPC), to organise a conference on direct action in 1999, where I was a speaker. An anthology of articles edited by Steven Best and Anthony J. Nocella, called *Terrorists or Freedom Fighters?*, included Wicklund's article and an updated version of the presentation I gave at UPC's conference (2004). It was at this conference that I heard for the first time the veteran Australian activist Patty Mark speak about what she called 'open rescues'. Karen Davis also explored the principles of open rescues in *Terrorists?* (2004).

In his study of civil disobedience, Tony Milligan defines open rescues as '(1) removing animals from the threat of serious harm by humans; (2) doing so for the sake of the animals themselves; (3) apparent illegality in the form of trespass, unauthorised entry and property seizure; and finally (4) little or no sabotage of equipment and infrastructure. It can be also open or covert' (117–18). In a variation of these four aspects, open rescuers may also document conditions in which the animals are kept and, whenever possible, offer food, water, aid, and perhaps veterinary treatment for sick or injured animals. The rescuers identify themselves on camera as they wish to document their role as witnesses to the animals' plight. Further, they are prepared to defend their actions, including possible charges of trespass, to law enforcement.

For me, open rescues were a revelation. Here, at last, was an approach, strategy, and action that embodied my key values in animal rights—and conversely brought into sharp focus what I felt was wrong with the other kinds of direct action engaged in by some animal activists. In addition to Freeman Wicklund's call in *Agenda* for the return of nonviolence as a key value in our action for animals, Patty Mark's development of open rescues with the Action Animal Rescue Team in Australia showed how the principle of nonviolence could be put into practice in innovative ways. Open rescues focused on the plight of animals and not on shadowy groups and anonymous activists. They showed advocates as caring sleuths witnessing and helping and not as terrorists who threatened people in the name of animal rights.

In my article in *Terrorists?* I explained why I thought highly of open rescues:

> They tell the truth about cruel practices toward animals by documenting them with videotape footage, photographs, and reports, which are used to educate the public, secure media coverage, and challenge appropriate authorities.
>
> They clearly demonstrate a compassionate attitude among the advocates toward the cruelly exploited animals by, for example, providing bottled water to dehydrated chickens in battery cages, which inspires others to think positively about animal advocates and the animal advocacy movement.
>
> They respect the property of others, causing the minimum amount of damage to gain entry, including leaving replacement locks if any have been destroyed.
>
> The truth telling, compassionate action, and demonstrated respect reveal the animal advocates' larger understanding of their actions. (Best and Nocella, 2004, 88–89)

Open rescues aren't without risk. Because animals are still considered property, the removal of the sick and/or dying from a farm or lab is considered theft. Because these institutions don't want the general public to know what's going on behind and within the wire mesh cages, walls, fences, and steel gates of their complexes, it's only possible to document what's taking place inside by trespassing or breaking and entering. These are illegal activities. Because the people doing this make no attempt to disguise themselves, they can be easily identified and prosecuted.

In recent years, particularly in the United States, efforts have been made to criminalise the documentation of the suffering—let alone the removal—of animals in any institution that uses them. Some people have been prosecuted as a result. It's my belief that these draconian and, in my view, unconstitutional laws are a direct result of the success of open rescues in drawing attention to the misery of animals in these facilities. Significantly, the stories in the media have not been about violent vandals or hoodlums wearing balaclavas but about the appalling conditions for the animals, the laws that the *institutions* were breaking and not the activists, and whether a decent society should tolerate such unconscionable behaviour from those companies in whom it has placed its trust.

MEN AND VIOLENCE

One final aspect of the commitment to nonviolence needs to be mentioned: the role of masculinity.

I hope I've illustrated throughout this book that being a vegan doesn't automatically make you a 'good person', since you can adopt the regimen for any number of reasons (such as a bizarre desire for bodily purity, or as a cover for an eating disorder, or to make yourself feel superior) that have nothing to do with living with more compassion or adopting the four key values. In a trope as well-worn as it's inaccurate (Berry, 2004, 33–34), many meat-eaters trot out the observation that Adolf Hitler was a vegetarian, as if somehow that comment were a thoughtful analysis of why someone may be committed to the health of the animals, the planet, and themselves.

Another frequent and tenacious meme—it would be giving it too much credibility to call it a line of thinking—is that not eating meat is somehow a sign of femininity, passivity, and weakness, and that, conversely, eating animal flesh is a symbol of masculinity and strength. In her writings, Carol J. Adams has explored this sexualisation of eating meat and the parallel animalising of the female body and its products in pornography and advertising (1990). With other feminist writers, she's also looked at male violence against women and animals—particularly, as I've noted, within the context of threatened or actual violence towards children and companion animals in order to control or terrorise the spouse.

Of course, women also eat meat and some women harm their significant others (both male and female), but the evidence of newspaper reports and studies of various sorts suggest that most violence is committed by men: whether it's against human beings or companion animals in the home, or hunting wild animals, or killing bulls in a ring, etc. For Adams and others, these acts of violence are functions of a patriarchal society where the male is defined by his lack of empathy with or concern for other animals, particularly domesticated ones.

'Males, in our patriarchal society,' writes the veterinarian Michael W. Fox, 'may well show more cruelty toward animals, or justify the same, because they close off empathy more than females when faced with others' helplessness and suffering' (64). He continues: 'Self-serving religious and political ideologies also impair the ability to empathize, notably such ideologies as: man's God-given dominion (over women, animals and nature)' (65).

At the beginning of his book *Brutal: Manhood and the Exploitation of Animals*, Brian Luke asks the reader to '[p]icture hunting, trapping, vivisection, slaughter, and animal sacrifice. Imagine them in concrete detail, even attaching faces and names to those who are killing animals. Now picture a demonstration against one of these institutions, again putting names and faces on the protesters. What do you see?' His response? 'Most likely you saw men killing and women protesting.'

Like me, Luke is interested in 'not so much why women oppose animal exploitation as why men support it' (1). As far as I'm concerned, compassion is not an attribute that's gender-based. It's something innate within us—nurtured by the education we receive, the values instilled in us by our family and society, and the choices we make in our lives. So why are members of my gender so apparently in love with violence?

One reason is surely because we're used to being in control and holding power. The corollary of this is that if that control and power are threatened, those used to being in charge lash out at those weaker than them. As a gay man, I'm aware of how I may be perceived by heterosexists as somehow feminised, and therefore less powerful; as a man, I'm all too aware of my own expectations of being the boss, of naturally commanding attention and respect, simply because my gender has for centuries been used to occupying the position at the metaphorical and actual head of the table.

In my judgement, if veganism and nonviolence are to mean anything beyond mere dietary preference and a noble and unachievable ideal, then they must grapple with our—by which I mean male as well as human—tendencies to wish to impose ourselves on others and manipulate them to do our bidding. We must be open to the possibility that we don't have all the answers, that humility and attention and inspiring others through our behaviour are as valid expressions of leadership as posturing, causing the most noise, or making snap judgements under the guise of decisiveness.

In fact, any commitment to veganism and nonviolence must be grounded in complete humility, simply because *ahimsa* is, itself, impossible: 'Man cannot for a moment live without consciously or unconsciously committing outward *himsa*', Gandhi said. 'The very facts of his living—eating, drinking and moving about—necessarily involve some destruction of life, be it ever so minute' (Borman, 1988, 185). Thus, to be a genuine vegan is to recognise the fact that one can never be vegan; to commit to nonviolence is to recognise how steeped in anger, disappointment, frustration, and simple pique we are as human beings—*and to continue to pursue nonviolence nonetheless.* I like taking Gandhi's paradoxical reconciliation of the pragmatic realisation that being a vegan in a meat-eating world is an impossible task with the idealism of creating a world founded on compassion, truth, nonviolence, and justice.

MAKING THE INVISIBLE VISIBLE

It's a sign of the ongoing development of the animal rights movement that we can no longer justify any action—no matter how ill-conceived, unstrategic, or self-defeating it might be—because it's 'for the animals'. Through our efforts to educate people and raise their awareness about the animal industrial complex, through our work to influence legislators and the passing of popular referenda around the world, and through an ever-increasing array of plant-based products that allow people to move to a diet that is increasingly being recognised as one that is best for the environment, the animals, and our health, the animal advocacy movement as a whole no longer needs to be defensive or feel that it has to fight its corner in order to be heard.

Our task now is to maintain and enhance our credibility as reliable witnesses and documenters of the awful conditions for animals in circuses, zoos, factory farms, research laboratories, and wherever else they're used. By making visible what's invisible, by focusing relentlessly on the conditions for animals and not our own self-aggrandisement or self-righteous indignation, and by being professional in our communications, strategic knowhow, and presentation to the general public, we'll be more likely to pass laws that implement and enforce effective regulations protecting animals from harm and banning behaviours that hurt them. Further, if the movement successfully and honestly frames animal rights as part of a progressive agenda of social justice and not as a competition among human interests, I believe that our chances for success will be that much greater.

Armed with truth, fortified with compassion, and committed to nonviolence, we can leave the Misanthropic Bunker and show the general public, proudly and without embarrassment, that they too share the Magical Connection, one that their everyday actions and society's institutionalised contempt for animals hides from them, *to their detriment*. We can illustrate, without exaggeration or fudging the facts, the truth that the violence we inflict on animals shares the same root cause as the devastation we cause to the environment and the misery we visit on our own kind—that the complex of ideologies (philosophical, political, and spiritual) that frame marginalised people, including women and children, animals and nature, as only resources for our instrumental use, has led only to more violence and alienation from our families, other species, our planetary home, and ourselves.

But first we must stop the violence: in ourselves, in our language, in our actions. Violence never prevents violence; it ultimately only leads to more, reshaping and compounding the problem, which re-emerges at a later date invariably requiring yet more violence to 'solve' it. Unless we do this, then our goals won't be achieved. This is why nonviolence is a key value for animal rights.

10

The Animal Rights Practice

I n 1980, Jim Mason wrote in *Agenda*, the forerunner of *The Animals' Agenda*, about the need for animal rights activists to go beyond their immediate impulses towards something deeper: 'Just as we made a commitment to self-purification and acted on it [by going vegan], we must now make a commitment to self-education and act on that to give ourselves a greater understanding of the politics, economics, history and culture of animal exploitation. This knowledge will be our most forceful tool in any campaign against animal oppression' (12).

What Jim meant by 'self-education' is a process by which we learn how to peel away the lies that conceal the truth about our contradictory relationship with animals. Since my first forays into the world of advocacy with Compassion In World Farming, I've been engaged in a continuous effort to educate myself about the intersections of animal activism with other social justice movements and the philosophical structures that support them. As I indicated in the chapters on truth, I knew that emotion wasn't enough to stop exploitation; nor was simply sitting home and theorising a practical strategy. I needed to develop an animal rights practice.

What do I mean by 'an animal rights practice'? We're familiar with the word 'practise' as a verb to mean exercising or training to learn something or engaging in or putting something into use. As a noun, a practice is a way of doing something that is conventional or customary; or a place of business or work. To practise is also doing the same thing over and over again in order to perfect how you do it. All these definitions fit my idea of an animal rights practice: as a way to describe animal advocacy as a professional calling in which I embrace compassion, truth, nonviolence, and justice.

Practice has a further meaning, however: as a discipline or engagement with a set of philosophical, spiritual, or moral ideas that lead to a deeper understanding of our role in the world and even our nature as human beings. A yoga practice, for instance, entails commitment to a group of positions that, in combination and over time, lead to greater physical suppleness, breath control, and—most importantly of all—a more profound understanding of the oneness of the universe, and nonviolence in particular. This meaning of practice also defines my notion of what it means to be an animal advocate.

An example of my practice is that I have, since I became a vegetarian in 1974, collected campaign materials, books, videos, photographs, and artifacts (e.g., buttons, posters, and display materials) about animal rights and related matters. The result after three decades is a large and, to my knowledge, unique archive with more than fifteen hundred books. The archive has come to represent in a tangible way my life in animal rights: not only as a repository of knowledge and insight from which I draw for my work and writing, but as a reminder to me that animal advocacy didn't start when I informed my mother that I was no longer going to eat meat.

It didn't begin with Peter Singer, or Ruth Harrison's *Animal Ma-*

chines (1964), or Donald Watson's founding of the Vegan Society twenty years before that. It wasn't invented by Shelley, Jeremy Bentham, the neo-Platonist Plotinus, or the Roman historian Plutarch. Even the Ancient Greek philosopher Pythagoras—to name another famous vegetarian from years past—probably learnt it from someone else, perhaps from one of the followers of Mahavira, the founder of Jainism. Countless individuals have contributed to keeping our mistreatment of animals before the public, whether they've been scholars and great thinkers, or ordinary activists like Camberley Kate, Amanda (my colleague at the culinary school), and me.

The extraordinary growth in interest in human–animal studies and animal ethics within universities around the world (especially in English-speaking countries) over the last few decades has been both the cause and result of the movement's expansion. Folks such as myself who weren't able to attend a university have been fortunate to be exposed to rich ethical argumentation through books and public lectures. (I remember how more than two hundred activists were almost visibly energised by a talk that Peter Singer gave on animal ethics at a Coordinating Animal Welfare meeting I chaired in London in 1983.)

This process has been essential to our growth as effective advocates. As Mylan Engel Jr. and Kathie Jenni write in *The Philosophy of Animal Rights*: 'By subjecting our beliefs, attitudes, and practices to critical scrutiny, we learn what our most deeply held values are—an essential first step toward acting in accordance with those values. When philosophy helps us to live our lives in conformity with our most deeply held values, it becomes a transformative experience' (7).

It's beyond the scope of this book to discuss the full range of theories available to animal advocates (see the bibliography for more), and we've already touched on three of them (utilitarianism, rights-based philosophy, and ecofeminism). Nonetheless, I believe it's worth exploring some aspects of animal ethics that have sometimes proved thorny for animal advocacy.

RIGHTS VERSUS CONSERVATION

One of the most contentious areas of animal ethics concerns the battles between environmentalists and animal rights advocates. Individuals and organisations that are interested in wildlife conservation are concerned with maintaining the viability (population numbers, genetic diversity, and habitat) of biotic communities. Animal activists in general don't look at species at a whole, but at the wellbeing of individual animals. Sometimes these values clash, such as when a species of animal that biologists consider to be invasive or nonnative threatens the survival of another species of fauna or flora. The environmentalists want to eradicate the animal; the animal advocate considers it unacceptable to kill an individual creature.

A utilitarian position, such as espoused by Peter Singer, would involve the weighing of the relative interests of all parties that might be considered sentient and resolve itself through determining how much suffering would be entailed through the various actions that might be taken. Should feral pigs be decimating an area of outstanding biodiversity, home to many species of plants and insects, the utilitarian would side with the pigs, since it would entail more suffering for the pigs to be killed than for the plants and insects to die out. This calculation might have to be revised if the victims of the pigs' rapaciousness were other mammals, who were also capable of sentience and therefore would suffer more in losing their life.

An animal rights philosopher such as Tom Regan would agree that the pigs should not be harmed, but would argue that the reason for their being left alone is based on their intrinsic rights independent of any weighing of relative degree of suffering or the number of animals undergoing it. This would remain the case if only two pigs were engaged in the destruction of hundreds of nests, dens, and coveys of rodents, birds, and rabbits.

An ecofeminist might wonder about the context of this debate: why were the pigs on the island in the first place? What was the philosophical, economic, or social reason for their introduction, and might stopping the farming or domestication of animals make such conflicts less likely in the future?

Each of these philosophical schools, of course, would no doubt make the case for a less drastic way of resolving the conflict—such as drugging and removing the feral animals, or giving them contraceptives to stop them breeding—rather than killing them outright. But each would seek to place some consideration of the individual animal within a debate that too often devolves into the abstractions of species and ecosystems.

RIGHTS VS. WELFARE AND REGULATION VS. ABOLITION

The necessity of balancing abstract principle with practical solutions has rarely been more contentious than in the argument between animal rights and animal welfare. As I've argued, this debate has preoccupied the animal protection movement for more than a century. It catalysed a good deal of the struggle over BUAV. The debate raged long before I got involved, too.

First, some definitions. When I use the term 'animal rights' I employ it both as a description of the non-instrumental rights of animals as defined by Tom Regan and as a collective term for the three traditions of animal ethics. Neither utilitarianism nor ecofeminism generally recognise rights, including those of animals, in their *ethical* systems, even though the use of the word 'rights' may appear in their literature. It perhaps reflects my interest in engaging the issue of animal advocacy in the broader public sphere that I most often use the phrase 'animal rights' to talk about the *political* and *legal* rights of animals, as much as morality and ethics.

As I've discovered in my interactions with advocates in the U.K. and the U.S., the term 'animal rights' has become loaded with sociopolitical meaning. In the U.K., for instance, the term used most often to describe efforts by animal advocates is 'animal welfare'. Generally, animal welfare is the view that animals do not have rights. They may be used for human purposes, providing they don't suffer unnecessarily. They can be killed, providing that it's done humanely. This is a point of view I reject.

What interests me is that when some (but not all) animal advocates in the U.K. use the term *welfare*, I believe they mean *rights*. There are a number of reasons for this paradox. Not only, in my judgement, is the understanding of animal rights philosophy among advocates not as widespread as it is among their American counterparts, but British activists have told me that, because some illegal and violent direct activities have been claimed explicitly in the name of animal rights, the phrase is now almost indelibly associated with this type of exploit. No doubt, this manipulation of language reflects the media and the animal industrial complex's selective use of rhetoric and sensationalism, but the confusion illustrates how essential it is that we always practice nonviolence and resist the temptation to engage in internecine squabbles that only provide our opponents with means to distort our contact with, and outreach to, the general public.

Beyond the quibbling over terms, the debate over whether we should seek regulation or abolition is a real one—one that we *should* be having, although with less rancour and finger-pointing. My position is quite simple: abolition is always preferable to regulation; however, both abolition and regulation pursued simultaneously are necessary.

In my paper 'Utopian Visions and Pragmatic Politics: Challenging the Foundations of Speciesism and Misothery', which was published in *Animal Rights: The Changing Debate* edited by Robert Garner (1996), I wrote:

> Eventually animal advocates must realise that success in the animal advocacy movement is not a question of deciding which is a more effective vehicle for change: a national society or a local organisation. They are both essential. Success is not a question of competition

between national organisations and grass-roots groups. Each has a responsibility to help the other. Nor is success a question of whether incremental measures that improve the welfare of animals are inimical to the preferred goal of abolition based on the rights of animals. No one has ever proven that a small step obviates a larger one. Success in animal rights is, however, a question of the mind-numbing quantities of individual animals whose suffering cries out to those who hear them. In order to hear those cries more clearly, animal advocates must reject the artificial constructions and selfishness that divide their movement. They must unite around a long-term strategy that balances our utopian vision with pragmatic politics. (Stallwood, 208)

The position I articulate here and elsewhere has led to some accusing me that I'm not an animal rights advocate, a term that we've already seen is riddled with confusion. They are wrong. I promote the abolition of animal exploitation and reject its regulation. I base my position on the sentience of animals and regard veganism as the moral baseline in animal rights. I reject violence and I promote veganism. I consider these positions not only compatible with a definition of animal rights consistent with the four key values but a practical and pragmatic way of leading to positive social and political change for animals.

I'm reminded of Frances Power Cobbe, the founder of BUAV, and framer of its mission: 'The aim of the Union is to oppose vivisection absolutely and entirely, and to demand its complete prohibition by law, without attempts at compromise of any kind' (Westacott, 1949: 204). These are stirring words—a rallying cry to fire up even the toughest abolitionist and animal-rightist—from a charismatic individual who adopted a fundamentalist position in order to hold fast to a heroic ideal.

Yet Cobbe was neither a vegan nor a vegetarian, and she's just one of many examples of individuals throughout history who held out an absolutist position in one area but compromised in other aspects of their life. Perhaps one day everyone will subscribe to an entire array of absolutist positions on the human and animal condition. But I'm not holding my breath, and I'm not entirely sure that I'd like to be among them.

We inhabit a world in which a universal absolutist ethics is not realistically achievable. I've already mentioned the danger of people becoming obsessed with perfection and finding fault with individuals and organisations trying to achieve reform. I've yet to find these individuals successfully implementing programmes to the same standards they demand of everyone else. In the end, the fundamentalist abolitionist view of animal rights is more about the need to be in the position of permanent opposition than actually building coalitions and the infrastructure that will take power.

Life is messy, complex, and difficult. We make compromises all the time. History demonstrates that most, perhaps even all, freedom fighters and social change agents were flawed or had moral blind spots. Martin Luther King Jr. (1929–1968) was a womaniser; Gandhi had dubious relationships with his grandnieces; Nelson Mandela (1918–2013) supported and may even have committed property damage. If these individuals weren't perfect, why should animal activists be? Focusing on the destination rather than the journey gets too many of us into trouble. Even the most assiduous vegan will have used (perhaps unwittingly) an animal product, even if it's the body of the ground-up animal in the tarmac they drive upon.

In the case of animal protection, I have even less control over determining what we might call a vegan outcome. I'm mindful that I may have to make political compromises along the way. I ask myself continuously how to balance the utopian vision of animal rights with the pragmatic politics of animal welfare. For the sake of the animals, I always take the side of rights over welfare; however, there are times, particularly in the political arena, when welfare or regulation is the only option available. As has often been said, politics is the art of the possible. Nevertheless, I believe that any compromise must always be situated in the context of ending animal cruelty and exploitation.

VEGELOMANIA

Finally, it's necessary to voice another hard truth about violence in the movement, one I've eluded to throughout *Growl*: we don't take good care of each other—professionally or personally.

In the course of my four decades in animal protection, I've worked, sometimes very closely, with leaders who were virtuous and selfless but still used people shamelessly. I've no doubt that other social justice causes have their fair share of charismatic martinets and self-appointed messiahs concerned to cleanse the temple of those they consider charlatans and time-servers because they've seen the light. Human conceit, liquored up with religion or politics and often both, has frequently and tragically led to the use of force, violence, and injury in the pursuit of truth. I freely admit that in the course of my time in the movement I've been wilfully confrontational. But it's one thing to challenge a set truth to reveal fresh insight; it's another to leave no room for humility, self-doubt, and alternatives to megalomania and arrogant self-righteousness.

Our lives and efforts are trivial and inconsequential in relation to the universe; yet within the universe we inhabit, how we live and the impact our lives have on others are uniquely significant. Further, our personal universe influences all adjoining universes. Consequently, our ordinary actions make an impact on everything everywhere. We cannot afford not to be generous in our expectation that everything may change, even if we may fear that nothing will. As Gandhi once said, capturing the paradox of our existence: 'Live as if you were to die tomorrow. Learn as if you were to live forever.'

III

JUSTICE

She referred to a matter that was a perpetual source of bewilderment to her—the extraordinary incapacity of the human race, in a world where the good is so unmistakably divided from the bad, of distinguishing one from the other, and embodying what ought to be done in a few large, simple Acts of Parliament, which would, in a very short time, completely change the lot of humanity.

—VIRGINIA WOOLF, *NIGHT AND DAY*

11

Helping People Help Animals

ollowing my resignation from PETA, I was once again unemployed and directionless. I knew I had to take time out for myself and recover from what had been a gruelling experience. Unlike in the period following my first firing from BUAV, I had responsibilities to honour, including financial. So for two years, while I tried to find my true self again, I consulted for a number of organisations that engaged me to evaluate their programmes, fund-raising activities, and corporate identities. These included the Physicians Committee for Responsible Medicine (PCRM), Vegetarian Resource Group (VRG), New England Anti-Vivisection Society (NEAVS), and Citizens to End Animal Suffering and Exploitation (CEASE).

I made the case to Dr. Neal Barnard, PCRM's founder, that he should no longer view his group as the doctors' anti-vivisection organisation. PCRM should become, I urged him, a reputable organisation led by a medical doctor who'd challenge modern medicine to do better, including critiquing animal research and promoting wellbeing centred on a healthy, vegan lifestyle. He did just that, and he has become one among a range of vegan M.D.s who have literally re-written the health and nutrition manuals that have introduced many folks to a cruelty-free diet.

During this period, I was closely following developments at *The Animals' Agenda*. I'd given up on the magazine because it was frequently inaccurate and unnecessarily confrontational with the movement it was originally established to complement and further. I'd let my subscription lapse, as had many other once-loyal readers. From the editions published in the early 1990s, it appeared that the magazine was in terminal decline. Two people saved *Agenda* at this critical time: Jim Motavalli and Peter L. Hoyt.

I met Jim Motavalli during my first visit to the United States in 1980, when I stayed with Jim Mason in Connecticut. The Jims were good friends. Motavalli was a local independent journalist who went on to become editor of *E*, the environmental magazine, which was co-founded by another of Mason's friends, Doug Moss. Peter Hoyt, who also lived in Connecticut, was a consultant specialising in circulation management for a number of independent magazines. He was *Agenda*'s circulation director. In 1992, Motavalli accepted an invitation from the not-for-profit organisation that published *Agenda*, the Animal Rights Network (ARN), to become its temporary editor. Peter agreed to continue with his duties and to assume temporary responsibility for the office. Motavalli and Hoyt kept *Agenda* in publication and the office open during what became a two-year transitional period.

One of the ARN board members was Ken Shapiro, executive director of Psychologists for the Ethical Treatment of Animals (PSYETA). Ken's and my path had crossed often throughout my time at PETA and I respected him for his insightful approach to tackling animal exploitation and his general thoughtfulness. He and I kept in touch during my time as a consultant, which included closely monitoring the developments at *Agenda*.

I had no interest in becoming the magazine's editor. I wasn't ready to make a full-time commitment to another animal rights project, even though I greatly believed in it. Nonetheless, when Ken told me that Jim Motavalli was no longer in a position to continue as temporary editor, I decided to apply. So, a full circle was turned from my time with Jim Mason, *Agenda*, and *CAW Bulletin* in the late 1970s to my installation as editor in chief of *Agenda* in 1993. My involvement with ARN and its succeeding organisation, the Animals and Society Institute (ASI), has been a substantial part of my life since.

Wayne Pacelle, the chair of ARN's board of directors, formally offered me the position. Wayne had a long history of involvement with the magazine. After graduating with a B.A. in history and environmental studies from Yale in 1987, he became an associate editor. He continued to write frequently for the magazine after he was appointed The Fund for Animals' executive director in 1989, at the age of only twenty-three. In our conversation, Wayne said he wanted to stand down from ARN's board so he could focus more on The Fund and its campaigns. Ken Shapiro succeeded him as chair and became someone I could count on for support and constructive criticism. Although ARN was the legal entity that produced the magazine, I functioned on a day-to-day basis as the magazine's publisher and editor.

Once again, I found myself learning new skills that complemented those I'd learnt as an executive director and campaigns director. Although I'd produced newsletters and magazines for every organisation I'd been involved with, I'd never been exclusively a publisher and an editor with the responsibility for generating a magazine. I grew to appreciate the difference between being executive director of an organisation and publisher and editor. With the former, my duties primarily consisted of helping an organisation function efficiently and effectively as well as directing its growth. This was also true for a publisher and editor. But, as I discovered from publishing *Agenda*, one had the opportunity to enjoy a sense of completion, which is something I rarely felt as an executive director. As an executive director I'd overseen events and projects that had their own lifespan, but publishing a bimonthly magazine soon got me into a routine of at any one time starting an issue, producing another, and putting a third to bed. It's hard to beat the satisfaction of holding in your hands a printed issue, hot off the press. Of course, soon enough you find the errors that crept in unbeknownst to you, in spite of your efforts to root them out. Then it's difficult to look at the same issue again without only seeing mistakes grinning back at you!

One further difference I would appreciate between organisations and publications had to do with their different relationship with truth, as they understood it. Both convey a point of view, but the organisation's job is to address an issue in order to further its mission, which gives it some latitude in how it presents its case. The challenge of the organisation is to make sure it doesn't lose credibility. A publication, notwithstanding its editorial perspective, also needs to maintain its credibility. In its case, however, accuracy and reliable sources of information are the watchwords. I didn't want *Agenda* to produce propaganda or rhetoric, so I encouraged writers to frame issues, make arguments, and present facts—whether in their investigative journalism, commentary, or analysis—accurately and thoroughly.

Although I'd worried about honesty and accuracy with the members' newsletters and magazines I produced for CIWF, BUAV, and PETA, I did so even more at *Agenda*. The magazine had to stand on its own terms as a credible and professional publication regardless of what anyone might have thought about animal rights. In fact, I wanted it to be read by people hostile to animal rights who'd find it difficult, if not impossible, to challenge us on any terms other than to say they disagreed.

I was well aware that ARN was essentially bankrupt when I took it on. This required me to rebuild an organisation as well as re-establish the magazine. I relocated the office from Westport, Connecticut, to Baltimore, where I'd been living since 1990. Peter Hoyt, whose expertise in circulation and business in general made him the magazine's unsung hero, took responsibility for closing the old office while I focused on opening the new one.

Jump-starting a magazine with no money and an organisation on the brink of collapse is not an ideal situation. Thankfully, many people and organisations kindly stepped in with donations and grants to help make up the shortfall in the budget. The largest source of income for commercial magazines is from advertising, which is why the editorial content of many publications is often indistinguishable from its advertising pages. *Agenda* was not a commercial publication and our editorial mission didn't obviously lend itself to advertising—especially in the 1990s, when relatively few commercial products for vegans existed. Raising revenue was a constant struggle.

The generosity of the magazine's readers and grants from like-minded organisations and foundations were vital in keeping us in print. Through thick and (mainly) thin our readers remained steadfast. I got to know many of them and thanked them personally for their continuing loyalty. I stay in touch with quite a few. I'm pleased to say that the revived *Agenda* became an entirely new publication for lots of readers unaware of its difficult history.

A SIMPLE EDITORIAL PHILOSOPHY

I situated *Agenda*'s commitment to animal rights within a programme of progressive social justice. I allayed the concerns of some who were worried that my appointment would mean PETA receiving a disproportionate amount of coverage by making sure the magazine didn't over-represent an organisation. Our slogan, prominently displayed as part of our masthead on the front cover, was HELPING PEOPLE HELP ANIMALS.

My commitment was to work with organisations and individuals I considered among the world's leading experts. Although I preferred to work with animal rights advocates, I understood it might not be possible to obtain expertise only from this source. I was fortunate to know many of the key players in the U.K. and U.S., and I already had firm opinions based upon my experiences on which experts and organisations I could work with and have confidence in. Each issue taught me further lessons about knowhow, trust, and cooperation. Although a few authorities were unreasonable, unprofessional, and uncooperative, most were professional and generous with their time and knowledge.

I'm pleased to say that throughout the nine years I published *The Animals' Agenda* it never once spoke in support of using animals in an exploitative manner or strayed from an animal rights philosophy. I still receive comments from people who tell me how much the magazine meant to them. They speak well of the quality of the production (once more, Lawrence and Beaven performed stellar work in the design) and its reliability as a source of information and knowledgeable debate. Any publisher or editor would be glad to hear this, and it's a testimony not only to the outstanding editorial staff—including Jill Howard Church, Rachelle Detweiler, Laura Moretti, and Kirsten Rosenberg—many of whom I continue to work with in other capacities or remain in touch with as friends, but to the many individuals and organisations who supported the magazine in various ways.

Everyone who wrote or contributed to the content generously donated their time and expertise or only had their minimal expenses reimbursed. Looking through back issues and the cover features we published, I'm reminded of some outstanding investigative reports and in-depth articles exposing hitherto hidden issues. In 'Never on Sunday: The Amish and Animals', Jim Mason uncovered the cruel practices of an otherwise peaceful Christian sect, while in 'The Debate Within', Carol J. Adams and John Lawrence Hill explored the relationship between abortion and animal rights. In 'Wastebusters: Cutting Government-Funded Animal Abuse', the magazine published reports from a number of animal organisations on multi-million-dollar projects funded by the U.S. federal government that involved animal cruelty and exploitation and which could be cut without adverse consequences either to the project or to the animals themselves. We included articles on animals as victims of land mines and the possibilities for social transformation in humane education. We also profiled young activists.

Jim Mason exploring the Amish and their attitudes towards animals in *The Animals' Agenda. ASI*

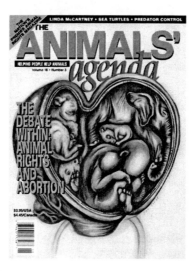

The brilliant work of artist Sue Coe was a regular feature of *The Animals' Agenda*, including the cover for our debate about animal rights and abortion. *ASI*

Whenever possible, I liked to add some humour to an otherwise serious subject. One of my favourite cover features was Mike Markarian's well-researched and clearly written exposé of fox hunting in America. I couldn't resist asking Lawrence and Beavan to produce a witty image of red-coated fox hunters on horseback with a pack of dogs on the White House lawn. We called the article 'Tally-ho, Dude!'

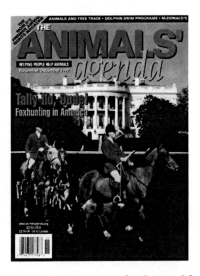

Lawrence and Beavan's photo montage of red-coated fox hunters on the White House lawn is one of my favourite covers. *ASI*

Two anthologies of articles emerged from *Agenda. Speaking Out for Animals: True Stories about Real People Who Rescue Animals* was an introduction to our complex relations with animals seen through the hearts and minds of individuals such as Paul McCartney, Anita Roddick, Maneka Gandhi (daughter-in-law of Indira), and Jeffrey Masson (2001). Jane Goodall wrote the introduction. It included selections from two of my favourite departments in the magazine: 'Happy Endings', a heartwarming collection of stories of rescued animals, and 'Unsung Heroes', profiles of ordinary people doing extraordinary things for animals. *A Primer on Animal Rights: Leading Experts Write about Animal Cruelty and Exploitation* (2002) contains our best investigative reporting and undercover investigations from some of the world's leading authorities. Jeremy Rifkin wrote the introduction and contributors included Sara Amundson, Gene Baur (then Bauston), Marc Bekoff, Karen Davis, Jim Mason, and Jill Robinson.

Even though many organisations helped us generously, they had their own publications they'd invested in and in which they promoted their own programmes and encouraged donations, which meant they were unwilling to promote *Agenda* to their supporters. Perhaps understandably, although I think short-sightedly, these house magazines and newsletters rarely made reference to any organisation other than their own, fearing it would result in donors learning about other groups and reassigning their financial contributions. Even though I'd tried to highlight the work of others in BUAV's magazine, I fully understood their point of view.

It's a continuing regret that *Agenda* was obliged to close, and I always wonder what might have happened if we'd received more support from the advocacy groups. I feel strongly to this day that *Agenda*'s editorial mission didn't compete with but complemented their publications. Everyone benefited from reading *Agenda* because it deepened people's understanding of animal rights and could build the movement, which would in turn only bring in more revenue to the organisations. The fear that someone might not support you because they discovered another worthy group felt parochial to me. The way to recruit and keep donors, I continue to believe, is to demonstrate leadership and accomplishment with outstanding programmes.

Before the blossoming of the Internet and social media, money was required for outreach through renting mailing lists and direct mail, as well as print and design. We never had sufficient funds in our budget to do this adequately. I envy those who now have multiple electronic means at their disposal to disseminate information efficiently and cheaply. In some ways, the Internet was the main reason for *Agenda* going out of business. Websites similar in style and content proliferated, although their content was sometimes either not new, or it plagiarised and misrepresented other people's work.

The final nail in the coffin was the economic crisis prompted by the tragic events on September 11, 2001. Many magazines, some with far greater resources than ours, ceased publication. In the best of times, people's concern for animals is limited, particularly when compared to such things as family and job security. After 9/11, animal rights became even less important for many. At a meeting of the ARN board of directors in 2002, we made the difficult decision to cease publication.

I had to resolve one outstanding matter before ARN and *Agenda* could end. When I'd taken on the magazine, I was disappointed to learn that my predecessors hadn't established an archive of books, files, photographs, artwork, and so on that I could use. I immediately decided to rectify the situation by founding what became the ARN Collection. We made it our policy to gather, sort, and archive every animal-related publication we received—including leaflets, direct-mail appeals, posters, audiovisuals, magazines, newsletters, and books. I asked organisations to make sure we were on their mailing lists as I didn't want to miss seeing anything they published. I pleaded with organisations not to throw anything away. All they had to do was to send me material they no longer wanted and I pledged to add it to our rapidly growing collection.

Several groups told me they'd thrown away valuable files and other materials when they moved because they didn't know what to do with them. I heard from another group whose archives were destroyed when a garden shed they were stored in burned down. Fortunately, I began to acquire archives from groups such as the Animal Welfare Institute and Argus Archives, as well as a unique acquisition from Claire Necker, a retired author of books about cats, who generously donated her outstanding collection of more than one thousand books about cats as well as more cat-themed artefacts than you could imagine!

At this time, Tom Regan retired as a professor of philosophy at North Carolina State University (NCSU), and the university established an archive in his name in Raleigh, North Carolina. The Regan archive is the only animal-rights university-based archive I'm aware of. Tom and I had been working closely together on a series of conferences co-ordinated by the Animals and Society Institute and Tom and Nancy Regan's Culture and Animals Foundation. This gave me an opportunity to visit Raleigh often and Tom kindly took me to NCSU to view the archive and to meet the archivists.

As much as I wanted to keep and build the ARN Collection, I reluctantly accepted that it had become an onerous responsibility to professionally maintain so large an archive. NCSU came to the rescue when we agreed to transfer ownership of the archive to the university as part of the Tom Regan Animal Rights Archive.

12

A Just, Compassionate, and Peaceful Society

At the time that *The Animals' Agenda* came to an end, the Animal Rights Network and I had been asking ourselves whether the magazine needed to change. Much had occurred during the twenty-three years of its existence. Was its mission still relevant at the beginning of a new millennium? If not, what should it be for the next twenty-five years? Moreover, what criteria should we use to answer this question? Was it sufficient solely to measure the movement's effectiveness by how far it had moved animal rights in public awareness? If not, how else could one evaluate, quantifiably and qualitatively, the progress of the movement?

To answer these and other related questions, I conducted my own research in consultation with my colleagues on the ARN board and outside the organisation. I read academic literature on social movements and political causes and pored over accounts by their leaders. It became clear to me that the animal rights movement had to confront some fundamental assumptions about how we saw ourselves and what we did, if we wanted to achieve moral and legal rights for animals.

One important source for reflection was *Eco-Wars* by Ronald T. Libby. In an informative chapter on the animal rights movement, Libby discussed the analysis of Bill Rempel, a research scientist at the Department of Animal Science at the University of Minnesota (62– 63). Rempel's bias was towards animal agribusiness, but he nonetheless was quite clear-eyed about the progress of animal rights, which he saw as passing through four stages: developing an issue, politicising the issue, legislating the issue, and litigating the issue. I liked Rempel's analysis, but thought it needed revision and adaptation to reflect more accurately my understanding.

The Five Stages of Social Movements

	Stage 1: Public Education	Stage 2: Public Policy	Stage 3: Legislation	Stage 4: Implementation	Stage 5: Public Acceptance
Maximum Influence					
Minimum Influence					

As a social justice issue progresses through each stage, its influence and resistance to setbacks increase proportionately.

My five-stage analysis of social movements [slide 1]. *Kim Stallwood*

I started at the end of the process—in a society in which animal rights are widely, if not universally, accepted—and worked back to our present time. From this exercise, I came to the conclusion that social movements, which sociologists define as a 'collective, organized, sustained, and non-institutional challenge to authorities, powerholders, or cultural beliefs, and practices' (Goodwin and Jasper, 2002, 3), pass through five stages, from public ignorance to public acceptance, as they journey from obscurity into the mainstream.

The five stages are as follows:

1. Public education: when people are enlightened about the issue and embrace it in their lives.
2. Public policy development: when the political parties, businesses, schools, professional associations, and other entities that constitute society adopt sympathetic positions on the issue.
3. Legislation: when laws are passed on the issue.
4. Enforcement: when laws are implemented and, if necessary, litigated.
5. Public acceptance: when the issue is embraced by the majority of society.

Simplistic though the five-stage analysis necessarily is, it functions as a somewhat blunt tool to help determine the current status of a movement, identify what remains to be done, and to determine strategy to achieve the stated mission. The schema offers a way to understand why social movements fail, stagnate, or succeed. In fact, not only does the model make it possible to determine the stage a social movement (or organisation or issue) has reached and what should happen next, but it allows us to know the future of that social movement (or organisation or issue). Even though some movements move between these stages non-sequentially, for any movement to achieve its mission it must pass through each of them and maintain an active engagement in each one. As a movement (or organisation or issue) expands its presence from stage one to five, while maintaining activities in each one, the power and control that any opposition may wield over it are progressively weakened.

The five-stage analysis confirmed that *Agenda*'s original public educational mission—to expose institutionalised animal exploitation and to nurture the modern animal rights movement—was the correct one. But stage two required us to refocus our mission towards public policy. Given our limited resources and the challenging economic times, we knew we weren't in a position to maintain the programmes in both stages, and many other fine organisations were already fully engaged in public educational activities, producing campaigns far more capably than we could.

Thinking further, we understood the five-stage analysis represented an individual's transition from moral crusader to political activist. Yet choosing to change one's lifestyle and creating institutional and societal change are very different tasks. We should never assume that if more individuals changed their lifestyles then institutional and social change would automatically happen. Human nature is capricious, whereas institutionalised regulations and laws are entrenched expressions of a society's values. Pro-animal public policy has to be fought for one law at a time, much as how we must convince one person at a time about animal rights.

Through the focus of my five-stage analysis, I concluded that *The Animals' Agenda* functioned in stage one (public education) and that we needed to move to stage two (public policy). So in 2002 we reinvented ourselves as the Institute for Animals and Society (IAS), the first animal rights public policy think tank.

Our vision for IAS was to be the 'recognized leader in the advancement of institutional change to establish moral and legal rights for animals as fundamental to a just, compassionate, and peaceful society' (IAS, 2003), with a mission to 'develop knowledge in the field of human–animal studies, support practices to address the relation between animal cruelty and other violence and promote action to protect animals through the adoption of ethical, compassionate public policy'.

Our work was strengthened when Ken Shapiro's PSYETA, which also functioned as the Society and Animals Forum (SAF), merged with our combined Animal Rights Network/Institute for Animal Studies to establish the Animals and Society Institute (ASI) in 2005. After I returned to the U.K. in 2007, I continued as ASI's European director. ASI is an independent source of credible expertise and accurate information, reflecting the depth and diversity of issues and philosophies in the animal movement. It's a bridge for scholars and students to educational programmes, advancing human–animal studies and animal advocacy. It offers an inclusive worldview on the moral and legal status of animals, fostering co-operation not only between the animal advocacy movement and other social movements and interests, but also within the movement itself.

WHERE WE ARE NOW

Since the heady days of the mid-1970s, the animal rights movement has not progressed beyond its public education phase of stage one. True, it has some presence in public policy, legislation, and enforcement (stages two through four), but animal advocates I think often feel more comfortable in the moral crusade (stages one and two) than as part of a social movement (stages three and four). Unfortunately, the animal industrial complex is deeply ingrained and fully engaged in all five stages, which is why much of the public debate and legislation relating to animals is about the parameters of how they can be used and not the abolition of practices or protecting animals from violence. Those who represent the animal industrial complex remain in positions of power and influence; they control the public policy debate about the moral and legal status of animals. Animals are still principally viewed as property and therefore disposable commodities in public policy.

The Five Stages of Social Movements: Hunting Act 2004

	Stage 1: Public Education	Stage 2: Public Policy	Stage 3: Legislation	Stage 4: Implementation	Stage 5: Public Acceptance
Maximum Influence					
	Moral Crusade		**Political Movement**		
Minimum Influence					

As a social justice issue progresses through each stage, its influence and resistance to setbacks increase proportionately.

My five-stage analysis of social movements [slide 2]. *Kim Stallwood*

In spite of Lord Houghton's wholly accurate and persuasive presentation almost forty years ago about the need to organise politically, the animal rights movement's present strategy of stressing public education and encouraging lifestyle changes ('Go vegan!') reveals our political naivety. Stage one is essential to build up a critical mass of interested citizens, but it must be part of an organised, strategic political vision or mission and not a random call for moral improvement. The few legislative successes the movement has achieved are only a small part of our overall endeavours; even the use of ballot initiatives in the United States to halt certain practices is ultimately an extension of earlier public education campaigns. I certainly don't want to dismiss these efforts, but I don't see the strategy that would accompany these victories to embed the values of animal rights in mainstream public policy and political discourse.

Animal advocates may not wish to hear it, but it should be obvious that, under the schema I've outlined above, the later stages of creating social change are likely to require balancing the pragmatic politics of animal welfare with the utopian vision of animal rights. Most, if not all, social movements struggle, sometimes unsuccessfully, with the conflict between holding out for perfection or practicing *realpolitik*, for abolition or regulation. The animal rights movement is no exception (Francione and Garner, 2010). This tension is often framed as an exclusive choice. I don't support this view. Both are needed to help the other achieve the change they seek. The challenge is to learn how to direct strategies that pursue both at the same time.

I don't discount how hard this task is. Perhaps that's why so many of us would prefer to breathe the clean air of a moral crusade for personal change rather than wade through the muddy and often turbulent waters of pragmatic public policy. To do the latter would also mean that the well-intended people who belong to the movement's numerous organisations, which are in turn led by charismatic individuals each pursuing their own vision and their own campaigns, must work together. This challenge isn't unique to animal advocacy. I know of no other social movement that has succeeded without some organisations and egos being willing to accept a subordinate role and delay the full implementation of their own vision in favour of specific targets and collective action.

One example where the movement did come together was over the issue of blood sports in Britain. The issue had been a divisive one in the U.K. for generations, and those who wished to bring an end to fox, stag, and deer hunting and hare coursing remained in the first stage of public education for decades, with occasional success in public policy (for example, some local municipalities opposed hunting on public land). Within the last couple of decades, many parliamentarians introduced private members bills (legislation that isn't sponsored by the government, and thus usually fails), which indicated that the issue of blood sports had moved to stage three. Finally, in 2004, the Labour government passed the Hunting Act, which in turn triggered stage four: enforcement. Pro–blood sports enthusiasts failed in their attempts to sue the government in the House of Lords and over the infringement of civil liberties in the European Court of Human Rights.

A decade since the passing of the act, the abolition of blood sports continues to enjoy public support (stage five). However, a law is only a law as long as the legislation is on the statute books and as long as it's enforced. At the time of writing the Conservative and Liberal Democratic coalition government is committed to bringing up a vote in the House of Commons on the future of the act.

Although far from perfect, the passage of the Hunting Act was something of a watershed in pro-animal legislation. It legitimised the public policy and legal position that hunting is a cruel and ineffective wildlife management tool that should be prohibited. The Act also empowered hunt opponents to shape public policy and had the strange effect of turning hunt proponents, who'd long derided 'sabs' and demonstrators as anti-social hooligans and law-breakers, into protesters and law-breakers themselves. The League Against Cruel Sports reports on its website that there have been 285 convictions under the Hunting Act up to 2012.

More significantly, the Hunting Act was the result of a multi-decade, multifaceted effort, largely started by Lord Houghton's 'Putting Animals into Politics' campaign during the general election in 1976. By establishing animal welfare, for the first time, in a manifesto or platform commitment made by the political parties, the animal advocacy movement in the U.K. signalled that it was ready for stages two and three. Hunting became a mainstream political issue. An important turning point came when the Labour Party won the 1997 election with an electoral landslide. Its manifesto committed the party to 'ensur[ing] greater protection for wildlife. We have advocated new measures to promote animal welfare, including a free vote in Parliament on whether hunting with hounds should be banned by legislation'. (See note on p. 204.) This meant that it was government policy, not the responsibility of an individual MP with a private members bill, to move forward any legislation on the issue.

Contrast the Hunting Act with other animal issues that aren't presently framed as legitimate public policy, such as the impact of breeding so-called pedigree cats and dogs on companion-animal overpopulation, or the promotion of the benefits of a vegan diet for human health, the environment, and as a mitigation of global climate change. If either of these positions seem to you only matters of personal choice or if you believe it's utopian that any party or governmental body would adopt these as public policy, then that illustrates how the issue has not moved from stage one. On the other hand, the ban on smoking in public places and legislation enabling gays and lesbians to form civil partnerships or to get married are significant developments in the public's understanding of contentious issues and show how relatively rapidly changes in public policy can be codified in legislation. I, for one, never thought I'd see them in my lifetime.

The animal rights movement should study these campaigns and other social movements and their coalitions to learn how they changed public policy and passed laws. To take one of the above examples, in the U.K., Action on Smoking and Health (ASH) works with, and receives funding from, the British Heart Foundation and Cancer Research United Kingdom. One of its strategic priorities is to 'press for concrete and evidence based measures to effect policy change and reduce the harm caused by tobacco.' Similarly, Stonewall, a relatively new organisation founded in 1989 in the U.K., develops ideas and policies to remove discrimination and to improve the lives of lesbians, gay men, and bisexual people. Stonewall's accomplishments include equalising the age of consent for heterosexuals and homosexuals, lifting the ban on gays and lesbians in the military, and allowing civil partnerships.

Although each social movement naturally involves at its heart uncountable individually transformative moments (e.g., people deciding to stop smoking and men and women coming out as gay), both ASH and Stonewall place more importance on public policy and legislation than most animal rights organisations do. ASH and Stonewall are no different from the animal rights movement in that they had to advance their issues through the five stages if they wanted to accomplish their mission. It's true that the animal rights movement is a uniquely altruistic movement in that its constituency has no voice, whereas ASH and Stonewall work for the benefit of their supporters and the general public at large. However, what ASH and Stonewall have accomplished over a relatively short period of time has been astonishing, and their achievements underscore the absolute necessity for the animal advocacy movement to situate animal rights within a strategy of progressive change that demonstrates the (human) benefits of animal liberation.

A 'free vote' is the name given to a procedure whereby MPs and Lords are allowed by their party enforcers, or 'Whips', to vote according to their conscience. Normally, Whips instruct MPs and Lords to vote along party lines. Free votes in Parliament are usually reserved for issues considered to be moral and that cross party affiliation and ideology—such as hunting, abortion, gay marriage, or the death penalty.

13

What Is Justice?

We've explored three of the four points on my animal rights moral compass. Truth guides us in our journey towards ethical relations with animals. Compassion shows us the path to those who need our help. Nonviolence is the light we follow in all our dealings with animals. We come now to my fourth key value. Justice brings together compassion, truth, and nonviolence to build the road we take to animal liberation. Compassion, truth, and nonviolence are justice in action.

Justice in relation to animals has three aspects:

- Equality: to ensure that the law recognises animals, like humans, as sentient beings in their own right in order for them to receive their due legal protection.
- Fairness: to require the law to protect animals, appropriate to their needs, as subjects of a life with inherent rights.
- Duty: to insist that individuals and society respect and enforce justice for animals.

Justice is usually something we feel the absence of—when we're denied it, through unfair and unequal treatment, or when we witness someone being subjected to discrimination or repression. Injustice is often a consequence of a prejudice based on a feeling of superiority (of gender, sexual orientation, race, or species). It occurs when we're indifferent to the plight of others (whatever their species), and fail to recognise the truth of their circumstances. Injustice can lead to violence, whether physical, verbal, or mental.

Although we may think of justice as an abstract virtue, available to every human being if all things were equal, the meaning of justice is in fact fully embedded in the cultural traditions of societies. It's subject to the influence of political, moral, economic, and religious values and realities. In other words, all things are rarely, if ever, equal, which means that justice isn't a given and must be fought for and continually protected against those who would seek to overturn it in favour of their own values and realities.

It's hardly necessary to highlight the many examples in history of injustice towards individuals, cultures, societies, and even peoples. Those in authority seize an opportunity to exert power and control over others to further their interests, which requires either the exploited group to speak out, or for others to do so on their behalf. Either way, claims for justice are challenges to authority; and all too often, the decisions about justice are made by those in power with control over others—which means that justice is often perverted, as well as delayed and denied, and why the fight for justice must take place in the political arena as well as within the moral or legal frameworks of society.

Justice is never won easily. Authority would prefer to ignore injustice rather than confront it. Power and control are never relinquished readily. The case has to be made; the work has to be done; people and their elected representatives need to be convinced, over many years, if not generations, and through several stages. This is the struggle that the animal rights moral compass should lead us through, to liberate animals from human tyranny. We are embarked on a campaign for justice for animals.

Our society rarely thinks of animals in terms of justice, or of our treatment of them as a form of injustice. We establish anti-cruelty statutes and laws and regulations encouraging humane attitudes and behaviour. In a handful of cases, prohibitions specifically outlaw cruel acts against certain species or in very particular ways. Notwithstanding these hard-won victories, our power and control over animals are absolute. We are their injustice. Indeed, I often think that how we treat animals is so immeasurably and unbelievably exploitative that we are beyond any scale of justice.

Thankfully, the idea of justice for animals is beginning to receive attention—not least because more of us are placing animal rights within the context of a larger commitment to social justice, such as for civil rights and gender equality. More are coming to the realisation that justice for animals and justice for humans are inseparable, interrelated, and mutually beneficial, and that simply to deny justice to animals when it's enjoyed by humans is speciesist. As the great humanitarian Henry Salt wrote in 1907: 'But if the principle which prompts the humane treatment of men is the same essentially as that which prompts the humane treatment of animals, how can we successfully safeguard it in one direction while we violate it in another?' (*Humane Review*, 8)

JUSTICE FOR ALL

What might justice—as opposed to simple charity or kindness towards animals—look like within the context of a society composed of laws that regulate competing interests and are underpinned by fundamental rights that protect the inviolability of the human person, private ownership, and an orientation towards freedom of conscience, association, and movement? Certainly, the utilitarian position radically asks us to consider in every ethical and practical judgement that, all things being equal, animals' interests are equal to humans, for instance in access to food, freedom from imprisonment, or the violation of their bodily integrity.

Both the utilitarian and rights position reject the critique, still commonly presented today, that animals cannot possess rights because they cannot articulate them or do not possess the full range of attributes that are commonly associated with rights-holders: self-consciousness, the ability to reason, etc. Those that speak on behalf of animals' interests and rights argue that human beings routinely assign rights and interests to humans who do not meet these criteria—particularly infants and people who are mentally impaired in some way. They point out that some animals possess greater mental capacity than these humans, and that it is a circular argument based on speciesism to claim, as some do, that these moral patients belong to a species that typically or normally would possess these criteria. In fact, we regularly provide particular rights to moral patients that may not be applied to moral agents. Why could the same not be the case for moral patients who happen to be nonhuman?

The 'argument from marginal cases', which is the unfortunate name given to the thinking in the previous paragraph, points to an important distinction between justice and charity. Many thinkers through the centuries—most notably Immanuel Kant (1724–1804)—have argued that it is good to be kind to animals. Kindness is a virtue, and to cultivate it on vulnerable animals is to develop an aspect of our humanity that is worthwhile in and of itself and would make that individual less likely to harm (more important) human beings later in life.

In a similar vein, charitable activity towards animals such as that practised every day by Camberley Kate is, I would argue, a vital reminder that we share fellow-feeling with animals, and that it is precisely because we recognise their need for shelter, food, love, care, and family *in ourselves* that we want to be around them and are drawn to them. Finding homes for companion animals, rescuing them from abuse or abandonment, and reuniting them after natural disasters with their family members are all expressions of that common bond, the Magical Connection, that we have with other creatures.

A justice-based solution is, like compassion, tougher and harder-edged than charity. If charity depends on individual good-heartedness, justice reflects the sanction (in both meanings of the word) of society and the enforcement of law and order. In the case of Camberley Kate, justice would mandate that living with a companion animal involves an obligation to care for that animal, and punishment if you don't: you'd have to spay or neuter the dog or cat, or else face a fine; you'd be punished should you abandon that creature. The distinction here is that justice would attempt to make a Camberley Kate unnecessary because our instrumental, throwaway attitude towards companion animals (and our reliance on altruistic individuals like Kate Ward) would be replaced by a justice-oriented relationship with animals, which would accept that they are members of a family and not property to be owned. They'd remain moral patients in that their reproductive cycles would be curtailed in their own interests—and in the interests of a broader human society, which would no longer have to take in unwanted cats and dogs and to suffer the horrors of mass euthanasia.

Domesticated companion animals are, perhaps, the most immediate and easiest targets for a justice-based reconsideration of our obligation to nonhumans. For other kinds of domesticated animals and animals whom we exploit for experimentation and leisure activities, we need to turn to political science for insight on how far the animal rights movement has to go to make the moral and legal status of animals a mainstream political issue.

I've already argued that injustice characterises our activities with animals. The animal industrial complex is injustice on a massive scale. Attempts to ameliorate the conditions for animals in these facilities—such as making sure the animals are unconscious when slaughtered or their cage-size is increased—don't address the injustice of the facts of their lives and deaths at our hands. Justice sits squarely opposed to an instrumental use of any being, even should some of those animals' interests be respected. Humane slaughter laws may in some perverse way be charitable in that they kill the animal more swiftly or with less violence, but they are not just.

In recent years, animal welfare science in the biological and veterinary sciences and animal studies in the social sciences and humanities have been presenting at times radically different visions of animal cognition and sentience than heretofore. The former work is revealing animals not merely to be 'subjects of a life', as Regan has characterised their cognitive realm, but creatures capable of forming cultures, languages, and an array of activities that point to a sophisticated form of self-consciousness. The latter studies are showing us how deeply embedded animals are in our social structures, our imaginations, and creative endeavours, and how (sometimes disturbingly) they are embodying our own pathologies in coping with our mutual animal natures.

These revelations about our animal brethren are paralleled in the emerging disciplines of animal law and political science around animals. In the United States, Australia, and Europe, animal law is enjoying significant growth in research and litigation (Radford, 2001; Schaffner, 2010; Wise, 2000); however, the study of animals and politics is less developed, although there are indications that this is changing.

For many years, Robert Garner has stood out as the primary political theorist exploring the political status of animals (1993, 1996, 2004, 2005a, 2005b). His current research considers society's treatment of animals within the context of justice and the application of ideal and non-ideal theory to animal ethics with respect to legislation regulating and ending animal suffering. Justice for animals should be rights-based but humans, he argues, have a greater interest in life and liberty. Nonetheless, the consequences for animals are far-reaching as many of the current ways in which animals are currently used would be viewed as unjust. New research in the political status of animals is being led by Siobhan O'Sullivan in *Animals, Equality and Democracy* (2011) and Sue Donaldson and Will Kymlicka in *Zoopolis* (2011).

O'Sullivan makes the case that existing inconsistencies within the law relating to animals should be addressed. For example, laws concerning dogs in the home and in the laboratory: one set refer to companion animals; the other, research tools; and the difference reflects the contradictory nature of how people view dogs. O'Sullivan argues that the law that establishes the highest standard of animal welfare should be applied consistently wherever the law relates to that species, regardless of the circumstances. In other words, we should treat the animal in the laboratory no worse than the law stipulates that we should treat the animal in the home. If we don't cut up our companion animal in the living room, we shouldn't do it in the lab.

Donaldson and Kymlicka apply political theories on citizenship to animals. They argue: 'Some animals should be seen as forming separate sovereign communities on their own territories (animals in the wild vulnerable to human invasion and colonization); some animals are akin to migrants or denizens who choose to move into areas of human habitation (liminal opportunistic animals); and some animals should be seen as full citizens of the polity because of the way in which they've been bred over generations for interdependence with humans (domesticated animals)' (14).

Each of these ideas challenges prevailing norms about the 'appropriate' or 'inappropriate' use and position of animals in society. And that is precisely the point: to present ideas that might alter our speciesist preconceptions about the proper place of nonhumans in 'our' society. If they seem wacky or unfeasible, it's because so little groundwork has been laid within the polity to reconfigure our relationships. The animal rights movement has vigorously claimed moral rights for animals. It now needs to persuade society and its representational governments to recognise *legal* rights for animals, which includes enforcement of those laws by the state.

Long a moral crusade, animal rights now needs to be a political movement as well, embedding itself fully within other social justice movements and drawing inspiration, support, and knowledge from the other activists. Advocates need to engage in these other struggles, not merely because it's the ethical thing to do, but because we need to show that our struggle is the struggle of these other social movements and their coalitions *as well*: that animal rights is their fight, too. We've long expressed our bafflement at how other social movements fail to 'get' that animal rights is a social justice concern. We need to *show* them that animal rights is also about fighting food insecurity, protecting the environment and biodiversity, and opposing sexism, racism, homophobia, and other forms of prejudice.

WE ARE THE PROBLEM AND THE SOLUTION

On the table in front of me lie three appeals for funds. The first is from a national animal rights organisation that promotes vegan, cruelty-free living, and exposes institutionalised animal exploitation with undercover investigations. The second is from an animal sanctuary, which rescues not only cats and dogs, but also farmed animals such as chickens, goats, and sheep. The last request is from a local refuge, which works in practical ways to help people, including their children and companion animals, who've been abused by their partners. Each one wants me to support their work by making a donation. But my funds are limited. It isn't possible to help everyone. Which one should I choose? Which is a priority?

These agonising decisions aren't unique to animal advocacy. Many movements for social justice present choices between achieving larger goals and making an immediate impact on the lives of individuals. We're all torn between campaigning to change a system and the desire to do something right now to make a situation less terrible. We try to weigh the needs, attempt to measure the successes of organisations, and ask ourselves what 'success' might mean, and in what context. At times, our funding only seems to generate more requests for funding, and changing the world for the better remains elusive, even illusory.

Because I've worked so long in the animal advocacy movement, I'm often asked about which organisations to support. My responses may be as hesitant and complex as the above conundrum implies. But I've found that my four key values in animal rights guide me on how to understand the problem of animal cruelty and exploitation and to determine effective ways to act for animals. I also find it helps in making a decision to remind ourselves that we, *homo sapiens*, are the problem and not the animals. They don't choose to subject themselves to the cruelty and exploitation we inflict upon them. We cause the suffering. We're also the solution. Animal rights begins and ends with us.

We are the reason why the animal rights movement is obsessed with moments of personal transformation. If only, we think, we can change people's attitudes, behaviour, and beliefs, as I changed mine, and you yours, then most likely we'll be able to change the hearts and minds of everyone else. If only *we* can make everyone see what I now see and go vegan, then we'll be able to hang going-out-of-business signs on zoos, slaughterhouses, research laboratories, and much more. We'll have accomplished our animal rights mission.

This is an attractive idea because it gives us immediate agency. It fires us up with evangelical zeal, provides us with focus, and directs our energies outward. It's also, as I've argued, a fundamentally limited approach. Not everyone will experience that connection we had with an animal. Not everyone will want to go vegan—or if they do, they won't maintain their diet and drift back to eating meat, eggs, and dairy products when animal suffering is no longer as important to them. However we may wish it otherwise, we must accept this reality. We cannot afford to wait until everyone has been converted. That's why, while individual change is good, institutional change is better.

THE ANIMAL RIGHTS FRAME

How many times have you found yourself saying 'There ought to be a law against [undesirable activity here]!?'

Well, there *should* be laws against abusing animals. Tougher laws, enforceable laws. These laws will obviate the need for personal revelations, moral shocks, or even the vaguest form of empathy. As Singer and Regan suggested decades ago, you won't need to care about or even like animals to treat them justly. Animals won't simply be the recipients of charity from the kind-hearted or the socially outcast. They'll receive justice. Laws not only reflect our society's norms, they also guide them. Statutes, vigilantly guarded and properly enforced, will establish a set of legal, moral, and *psychological* conditions that will change society in such a way that it won't only be illegal to harm an animal, but it'll also be immoral, and socially unacceptable, even deviant to do so.

After forty years of the modern animal advocacy movement, it's time to move beyond the stage-one formulations of media stunts, information dissemination, demonstrations, advertising campaigns, and personal appeals by celebrities to stages two and three. Certainly, we can continue to influence public opinion to be more sympathetic to animals, but we need plans that are less whimsical, harder-headed, more strategic, and more directed. We need to be unafraid of power.

As it is, animal advocates are boxed in. We're frightened of being told by other social justice movements that animals aren't as important as humans. We're frightened that we'll be called sentimental or irrational or self-righteous or just plain weird. We're frightened that others won't be as committed or absolute or uncompromised as we are. We're frightened that, when push comes to shove, the politicians will let us down because we're supposedly one-issue voters, and that issue just isn't important enough.

Well, these are the risks that any movement has to take as it grows up. It has to expect vilification and opposition. We have to expect to be called 'radicals' and 'terrorists' and a whole host of even more unpleasant names. What we do is hold on to the four key values and not only won't we earn those labels, but the general public—whom I genuinely believe is more open to our cause than we advocates imagine—will stick those labels on those who oppose us.

Fortunately, most of us live in societies where the free exchange of ideas and the right to petition the government and elect one's representatives are givens. True, moneyed interests and powerful lobbies exist that make it hard to get through to legislators. So start small and start locally. Pick an issue, analyse the problem, and propose a solution. Attend your local council or ward meetings. Bring in experts, write policy papers, give money, hold fundraisers. Organise, campaign, join a political party, run for office yourself. Show the politician you have a constituency; do the same with other groups in your area. Build bridges, develop a network, make animal advocates an unavoidable part of the constituency that supports a candidate.

RESILIENCE AND SOPHISTICATION

The animal rights movement differs significantly in two ways from other social justice movements. As Robert Garner explains: '[F]or humans to campaign on behalf of [animals] requires an altruism that is much more profound than for other social movements. Not only does it involve action to seek the advancement of the interests of another species, there is also a potential conflict between the interests of animals and those of humans' (2005b, 164).

Animals cannot organise themselves into their own social movement or be the agents of their own liberation. We have to do it for them, on their behalf. This onerous responsibility makes it even more important for us to understand how to achieve animal rights. If we are to be serious, we'll also have to recognise the benefits we accrue from our exploitation of animals. I happen to think the animal industrial complex overstates these benefits, just as it underplays or ignores the considerable costs. But we need to admit that much of the public remains reluctant to give up any pleasures or entitlement (e.g., eating meat) even though these pleasures may in fact be negative and the entitlement a burden on the body politic.

Here, too, the animal advocacy movement will need to be resilient and sophisticated. All progressive social movements have met with claims that, should their particular goal be realised, civilisation will collapse, the economy will tank, and all progress will come to a grinding halt. The animal industrial complex will continue to pit one social group against another in an effort to deflect attention away from its massive and systemic destruction of sentient beings.

In the end, however, the fundamental task of the animal advocacy movement is to be pragmatic and visionary. When Lord Houghton told us at the symposium in Cambridge in 1977, that animal welfare was a 'matter for the law [which] means that to Parliament we must go [because that] is where laws are made and where the penalties for disobedience and the measures for enforcement are laid down' (Paterson and Ryder, 1979, 85), neither he nor I could have imagined the options that are now available to those who want to live a cruelty-free, vegan life. In a few years time, non-animal based models may have taken the place of all creatures in laboratories and the circuses that use animals will no longer exist.

I certainly recognise how rapidly economic circumstances and technological development can change the political and social landscape, and how it has done and will do in the future for animals. But that doesn't mean we don't need to take Lord Houghton's advice very seriously and get involved. Animals are already in the political arena, except these representatives are allied with powerful commercial interests—the animal industrial complex—to ensure that animal exploitation continues for as long as possible, *even when non-animal products, services, and options are available.* Their involvement in the political process helps to maintain the status quo, to make sure that any regulations or laws protect their interest in using animals rather than further our interest (and the animals' interest) in not being used at all.

I closed Chapter 6 with the observation that I hadn't realised by the time I returned to live in the U.K. in 2007 that the U.S. animal rights movement would lead the world. When I left for the U.S. in 1987, I believed the U.K. animal rights movement was preeminent and would remain so. I'm fortunate to have played a role in the U.S. animal rights movement at a key time in its development. My view about this period in the movement's history may seem even more surprising given that during these intervening twenty years the British Parliament and the Scottish Assembly passed legislation making it illegal for packs of dogs to kill wildlife. To put this into perspective, such a move is akin to the U.S. Congress abolishing rodeos.

Notwithstanding these important legislative milestones in wild animal protection, I'm disappointed that the accomplishments we had achieved in the 1979 and 1983 general elections in positioning animal welfare as a mainstream political issue by, for example, the inclusion of animal welfare in the manifestos, were not used by the U.K. animal welfare movement as a foundation during the twenty years I was in the U.S. (1987–2007). To be sure there were other notable legislative achievements, including in the European Union, but the fundamental strategy of embedding the values of animal rights in the philosophy and agenda of change for the political parties was overlooked.

The 2005 general election campaign, in which only lacklustre attempts were made to place animal welfare in front of the parties and the electorate, confirmed my concern. It was largely a social media campaign involving a centralised system to email candidates while failing to mobilise voters to get active in their constituencies. At the same time, the campaign emphasised the importance of the participating national organisations to do all the necessary lobbying work at the national level. This isn't my idea of democracy in action. The 1979 and 1983 campaigns placed equal importance on conveying our message simultaneously at the local and national levels. Locally, we wanted organised activists to attend meetings in their constituencies with candidates and personally ask them for their support for our demands while the national groups lobbied for national policies on the same issues. Further, the strategy to organise within each of the political parties by encouraging animal activists to join and get involved to advance animal issues was missing in action. To Parliament we must go for animals in every country, in every election, locally and nationally.

Although these differences between the the U.S. and U.K. may be cultural and political, I am optimistic for the future of animal rights in the U.S. because of the strength of the third branch of government—the judiciary—and the ability to develop public policy through the courts. Such initiatives as the Nonhuman Rights Project and others led by the Animal Legal Defense Fund and The Humane Society of the United States in the courts and at the ballot box show promise. Surely the next step is a campaign to embed the values of animal rights within the policies of the political parties themselves so that when representatives are elected they're already committed to advocating and legislating for animals.

The hunting legislation in the U.K. was significant because it reversed the roles of animal advocates and those who enjoy killing wild animals for fun. Whereas hunting was lawful, protesting against the hunt, and particularly hunt sabotage, were viewed by the state, including law enforcement, as close to breaking the law. Now, hunters are at risk from breaking the law, with the protesters and hunt saboteurs fulfilling new roles as monitors ensuring that the law is upheld, which in turn leads to successful prosecutions. This reversal—from protesters to enforcers of the law—is one that animal advocates should generally aspire to whenever and wherever animals are exploited. The transformation is also reflected in the animal rights movement emerging from a moral crusade to becoming a social movement with political clout. This development from public education to public policy is reflected in my work with the animal rights movement as it has developed over the last four decades.

Regardless of whether our focus is the movement in the U.K., the U.S., or elsewhere in the world, animal advocates everywhere face similar challenges and opportunities. For example, I firmly believe we will witness in the not too distant future the collapse of factory farms or as they're now increasingly called, Concentrated Animal Feeding Operations (CAFOs). The resources CAFOs consume (grains, cereals, electricity, water, antibiotics, petrochemicals in the form of pesticides used to grow the feed for the animals, etc.) and the energy needed to operate them are disproportionate to the amount or quality of food they produce. This unsustainability will inevitably result in their demise. Together with the development of *in vitro* or cultured meat products as a healthier and economic alternative, I foresee a future when factory farms will be a much regretted chapter in our history. I'm only sorry that Peter and Anna Roberts won't be alive to see this day.

My belief in the end of factory farming doesn't mean the animal rights movement can sit back and wait for the collapse of the animal industrial complex. But it does mean that we must become more resilient and sophisticated in our approach. Our case for animal rights cannot simply rest upon the animals' plight. Nothing happens in a vacuum and animal rights is no exception. It's our responsibility to deepen our understanding of animal cruelty and exploitation as more than just their suffering.

As I have stressed throughout *Growl*, there are important issues related to understanding animal rights *as a class issue*—an aspect that the movement has insufficiently addressed. When I look around at the animal rights movement in the U.K. and the U.S., I see a largely white, middle class, affluent, and educated group of people who care passionately. We need to do much more to understand how to relate animal rights to the lives of ordinary, working people, some of whom are disengaged or disenfranchised from society. My response to this, and every, challenge remains to understand animal rights through the moral compass of the four key values of truth, compassion, non-violence, and justice.

Looking back over my four decades of involvement with the international animal rights movement I have the advantage of watching organisations emerge, succeed, and, in some cases, stagnate and fail. Similarly, I have witnessed charismatic pioneers become entrenched leaders protecting the interests of their organisations and in so doing become conservative in outlook, despite their nominally radical stance. In some cases, I recall their criticism of a previous generation of leaders whom they now come to resemble! All this speaks to the issue that for social movements to thrive and succeed they must continuously reinvent themselves while staying true to their missions. We need to recognise the ambivalence inherent in holding power and wielding control over any type of institution. As I witnessed particularly with BUAV but with others too, organisations have life cycles, including periods of activity and inactivity, and clarity and purpose.

As Tom Regan notes in *The Case for Animal Rights*:

Not only are animals incapable of defending their rights, they are similarly incapable of defending themselves against those who profess to defend them. Unlike us, they cannot disown or repudiate the claims made on their behalf. That makes speaking for them a greater, not a lesser, moral undertaking; and this makes the burdens of one's errors and fallacies when championing their rights heavier, not lighter. (1983, xiv)

Conclusion

My involvement with animal rights was motivated by my outrage at animal cruelty and exploitation. It was also an integral part of my psychological struggle with the expectations I had of myself as a gay man. These expectations were created, nurtured, and reinforced by me, my family, my friends, and by others as well as more broadly by society, although in the end I was answerable to no one but myself. Over many years, the more I understood what animal rights meant—morally, politically, and spiritually—the more I was able to connect with a sense of compassion about myself. This, in turn, helped me to connect with others. The Magical Connection with Boobaa and Honey was the emotional bond that gave me permission to like myself.

Although Gary and I never had as many rescued dogs in our home as Camberley Kate, I wonder now if my bond with Boobaa, Piggy, Beano, and Honey brought me full circle back to what I witnessed in my childhood. Have I become a contemporary Camberley Kate? Clearly, there are some similarities, principally a lifetime dedicated to helping animals, a predisposition to grumpiness, a steadfast commitment to following the moral compass we've made for ourselves, and a disdain for the views of others. Nonetheless, underneath our melancholic veneer beats a compassionate heart committed to helping others. Moreover, I don't think we're unique, as there's some of Camberley Kate in every animal advocate. I'd like to think that if Camberley Kate were alive today she'd be recognised by the animal rights movement as the unsung hero that she truly was.

My involvement in the movement helped me see that I could be connected with the world; that veganism was more than just the food I ate or the clothes I wore, or the things I filled our house with. It was also about living compassionately, honestly, nonviolently, and justly. Certainly, vegans can be proud of the number of animal lives we've saved and our contribution towards a peaceful world. But we also need to be kind to ourselves, reach out to others, take ownership of our power, and feel confident in our vision.

I say this because I was not always kind or considerate either to myself or others. I sat in judgement and pointed fingers, and espoused ideas that were the opposite of the key values I've discussed in this book. That is why this is the book that I wish Kim the Vegelical or Kim the Chef could have had all those years ago.

It's my sincere hope that, as you travelled along this journey with me in this book, you've discovered why animals are important to *you*, and that you are therefore more knowledgeable and better prepared to make a difference for animals than I was.

Where do we go from here? What are the next steps that we take? These are for you to decide.

Acknowledgements

It's often said—and it's true—that writing is a lonely process. Writing this book, however, has been a far from exclusively solitary experience. I recalled, as I wrote, encounters along the way with many brave, caring, and thoughtful people. Indeed, I've been very fortunate to meet, know, or work with some of the world's leading animal advocates in the modern animal rights movement. It's true that these encounters ranged from the inspirational to the confrontational. Nevertheless, they influenced me in some way or taught me something important.

Growl was in preparation for many more years than I care to admit. The project evolved considerably over time. Writing it was a relatively recent development. Indeed, I don't believe it would have been possible to write this book until a few years ago. I needed time, distance, and contemplation to look back with a constructive but critical eye.

As this book developed, friends, and colleagues advised, encouraged and, when necessary, cajoled. These conversations inspired me more than these individuals will ever know. I'm grateful to them and to so many people that it would be impossible to list them all here. This book couldn't have been written without them, including possibly you. Thank you!

In particular, I wish to thank Carol J. Adams (especially for introducing me to Scrivener!), Steve Baker, Batya Bauman, Hilly Beavan, Rod Bennison, Jeanne Daniels, Davy Davidson, Patricia Feurer, Ken Feurer, Robert Garner, Caryn Ginsberg, Marguerite Gordon, Che Green, Joel Kanoff, Hilda Kean, the late Marti Kheel, Anthony Lawrence, Sue Leary, Barb and Greg Lomow, Philip Lymbery, Mia MacDonald, Susan McBride, Carol McKenna, Cindy Milburn, Simone and Jack Patterson, Tom and Nancy Regan, Syed Rizvi, Richard D. Ryder, Patty Shenker and Doug Stoll, Debby Tanzer, John Thompson, and Darren Tossell. I am particularly grateful to my 1980s flatmate, Maureen Weir, who graciously gave me permission to include photographs taken by her deceased husband, Duncan. I also wish to thank the photographer Paul Knight for his creative and professional contribution.

My colleagues at *The Animals' Agenda* magazine and at the Animals and Society Institute deserve special credit. They earn a round of applause, as I'm not always the easiest of people to work with. Heartfelt thanks to Jill Howard Church, Rachelle Detweiler, Bee Friedlander, Peter L. Hoyt, Suzanne McMillan, Laura Moretti, Kirsten Rosenberg, Ken Shapiro, and Jacque West. I want to also express my appreciation to everyone who served, and is serving, as a director on the board as well as each and every individual, like-minded organisation, and foundation who supported in many different ways *The Animals' Agenda* and ASI. A bigger thank you to those who continue to do so!

I was very fortunate to recruit a small group of readers who generously gave their time and expertise reading drafts of this book. They read the manuscript once and sometimes twice. Their insight was invaluable. Their patience was tested with my repeated questioning. Of course, any fault herein is mine. Many thanks to Ian Bergin, Sebastiano Cossia Castiglioni, Jill Howard Church, Sue Coe, Rachelle Detweiler, Bee Friedlander, Julia Knowles, Barb Lomow, Norm Phelps, and Ken Shapiro.

Sue Coe and her creativity are constant inspirations. Sue always reminds me why I must never stop asking, 'Why do things have to be this way?'

Friends and colleagues, Sebastiano Cossia Castiglioni and Jane

Patterson, inspire me with their vision of a world made real with justice, compassion, and integrity.

Applause to everyone at Lantern Books. Martin Rowe patiently waited for me for many years to write this book. His advice and encouragement were invaluable. Special thanks also to Kara Davis, Gene Gollogly, and Wendy Lee.

As is evidenced from her brief appearances, Virginia Woolf is a writer whom I admire and is an inspiration.

Although Gary Baverstock does not feature prominently by name in this book, his presence in my life is the most important.

My life and its circumstances, including responsibilities and travel commitments, don't permit me to live with as many dogs as Camberley Kate. But there's one thing I am sure about. There can be no doubt that each one in her charge meant as much to her as mine do to me.

Whereas Piggy and Beano and Boobaa and Honey live forever in my heart, and with me in spirit in my animal rights practice, Shelly, a rescued Jack Russell who was found as a puppy at a Shell gas station in Virginia some twelve years ago, now shares my life.

As I complete this book, Shelly wants you to know her friends are counting on us to make a difference.

Me and Shelly. *Paul Knight*

Reader's Guide

PART I. TRUTH AND COMPASSION

1. How different are compassion, sympathy, empathy, and pity?
2. Is compassion for oneself essential before feeling compassionate towards others?
3. Discuss the positive and negative attributes of a vegelical.
4. How would you make the case for animal rights to yourself before you became aware of animal cruelty and exploitation?
5. Compare and contrast the moral and legal status of humans with that of animals.
6. Is it permissible to lie to further animal rights?
7. Is time in the Misanthropic Bunker time well spent?
8. Are you a Davincian, Damascan, Muddler, or Caring Sleuth? Explain why.
9. Discuss any personal transformative moments you may have experienced.
10. Do you consider yourself to be an advocate for animals? Describe what being an animal advocate means to you if you are or are not.

PART II. NONVIOLENCE

1. Are all Magical Connections the same?
2. Is violence to humans and violence to animals the same?
3. How do you understand the relationship between nonviolence and veganism?

4. Where do you draw the line between acceptable and unacceptable publicity stunts for animal rights? Explain why.

5. How would you describe your animal rights practice?

PART III. JUSTICE

1. Is animal rights a moral crusade or a social movement?
2. Why is justice important in establishing moral and legal rights for animals?
3. Is it possible to legislate justice for animals?
4. What do each of the three traditions—utilitarianism, rights-based philosophy, and ecofeminsm—in animal ethics say about animals and justice?
5. Describe a society that embraces justice for animals.

Notes

p. 9:   'In 1851, he was the first to be interred at St. Michael's Church'. Information about John Stallwood taken from the following: 'Almost-Full Graveyard Could Lead to Re-use'. <http://www.getsurrey.co.uk/news/s/2089675_almostfull_graveyard_could_lead_to_reuse>; 'Grave 1 John Stallwood'. <http://audioboo.fm/boos/830447–grave-1–stmikescamb-camberley-john-stallwood>.

p. 11: 'Her work with animals started when she took home a lame greyhound'. Information about Kate Ward taken from the following: Guy Pelham, 'Camberley Kate Dies', *Star* (August 9, 1979); Naseem Khan, 'Camberley Kate', n.d. Unidentified; <http://www.surreyheath.gov.uk/leisure/tourism/shm/camberleykate.htm>.

p. 20: 'Aldershot's slaughterhouse was at the time'. Information about the chicken slaughterhouse in Aldershot taken from the following: Andrew C. Godley and Bridget Williams, 'The Chicken, the Factory Farm and the Supermarket: The Emergence of the Modern Poultry Industry in Britain' (Reading: Henley Business School, University of Reading, 2007), <http://www.henley.ac.uk/web/FILES/management/050.pdf>.

p. 27: 'Later that month, we learnt'. Information about the *Open Door* programme produced by the Vegan Society taken from the following: <http://www.youtube.com/watch?v=rNskRUJRnrU&feature=relmfu>; <http://www.vegansociety.com/about/hall-of-fame/kathleen-jannaway.aspx>; and <http://www.vegansociety.com/resources/magazine/Back-issues.aspx>.

p. 31: 'In November 1944, when victory over Nazism was far from certain, Watson published'. Information about the newsletter taken from the following: <http://www.vegansociety.com/uploadedFiles/About_The_Society/Publications/The_Vegan_magazine/Feature_Articles/1944–news.pdf>.

p. 37: 'A well-planned, healthy vegan diet'. Information about the National Health Service taken from the following: <http://www.nhs.uk/livewell/vegetarianhealth/pages/vegandiets.aspx>.

p. 37: 'And the American Dietetic Association considers veganism'. Information about the American Dietetic Association's statements on a vegan diet taken from the following: <http://www.eatright.org/about/content/aspx?id=8357>.

p. 46: 'The term was first explored by the anthropologist Barbara Noske'. Information about Richard Twine's article taken from the following: <http://www.thescavenger.net/animals/the-iindustrialisation-of-animals-where-are-the-ethics-89912–538.html>.

p. 47: '8 billion chickens, 232 million turkeys'. Information about the number of farmed animals in the United States taken from the following: <http://www.humanesociety.org/news/resources/research/stats_slaughter_totals.html>.

p. 47: 'Globally, the world sucks 14 billion finned fish and 40 billion shellfish'. Information about the number of finfish and shellfish consumed in the United States taken from the following: <https://docs.google.com/file/d/0Bzm1dJXWcgufUWtoVHViR1JLY2c/edit?pli=1>.

p. 47: 'Six to eight million of them'. Information about the number of companion animals in the United States taken from the following: <http://www.humanesociety.org/issues/pet_overpopulation/facts/overpopulation_estimates.html>.

p. 48: 'A more immediate way to grasp this orgy of violence'. Information about the number of animals an average U.S. meat-eater consumes taken from the following: <http://animaldeathcount.webnode.com/>.

p. 78: 'By way of establishing my bona fides'. Information about the announcement of my arrival at Compassion In World Farming taken from the following: 'New Appointment', *Ag Scene: The Journal of Non-Violence in Agriculture*. Petersfield, Hants: CIWF. 1976. No. 43. December, page 15.

p. 101: 'One day, Fay told me that she planned to buy a fur coat'. Information about Fay Funnell taken from the following: Roger Tredere, 'Why Fur Coats Are An On-Off Thing: The Trade Says Business Is

Better, But Roger Tredre Doubts that the British Will Buy', *Independent* (January 22, 1993).

p. 132: 'As it turned out, some eight years after I departed PETA, Alex himself concluded'. Information about the interview with Alex Pacheco taken from the following: 'The Direction Peta Has Taken' (April 11, 2011) <http://animalrightszone.blogspot.com/2011/04/direction-peta -has-taken.html?spref=tw>.

p. 134: 'For example, PETA donates unwanted fur coats'. Information about PETA taken from the following: 'Why does PETA give fur coats to the homeless?' <http://www.peta.org/about-peta/faq/why -does-peta-give-fur-coats-to-the-homeless/#ixzz2pKuaTkBt>.

p. 135: 'This action is not only insensitive for economic and class reasons'. Information about the homeless in the U.S. from the following: 'The National Council for the Homeless—Minorities and Homelessness', <http://www.nationalhomeless.org/factsheets/minorities .html>.

p. 199: 'Our work was strengthened when Ken Shapiro's PSYETA'. Information about the Mission Statement of the Animals and Society Institute taken from the following: <http://animalsandsociety.org /pages/our-mission-and-vision>.

p. 202: 'An important turning point came when the Labour Party won the 1997 election'. Information about the Labour Party Manifesto in 1997, taken from the following: 'New Labour Because Britain Deserves Better' <http://www.labour-party.org.uk/manifestos /1997/1997–labour-manifesto.shtml>.

Bibliography

Adams, Carol J. 1990. *The Sexual Politics of Meat*. New York: Continuum.

———. 1994. *Neither Man Nor Beast*. New York: Continuum.

———. 2001. *Living Among Meat Eaters*. New York: Three Rivers Press.

Adams, Carol J. and Lori Gruen, eds. 2014. *Ecofeminism: Feminist Intersections with Other Animals and the Earth*. London and New York: Bloomsbury.

Animals' Agenda, The. 1995. Jim Mason. 'Never on Sunday'. Baltimore, Md.: Animal Rights Network 15, no. 5, pp. 20–24.

———. Various authors. 'Wastebusters: Cutting Government-Funded Animal Abuse'. Baltimore, Md.: Animal Rights Network 15, no. 5, pp. 22–26.

———. 1998. Carol J. Adams and John Lawrence Hill. 'The Debate Within: Animal Rights and Abortion'. Baltimore, Md.: Animal Rights Network 18, no. 3, pp. 22–27.

———. 1999. Mike Markarian. 'Tally-ho, Dude!' Baltimore, Md.: Animal Rights Network 19, no. 6, pp. 22–27.

Baker, Steve. 1996. 'We Need a Philosophy of Generosity'. In *The Animals' Agenda* 16, no. 5, pp. 44–45.

Batt, Eva. 1976. *What's Cooking?* Enfield, U.K.: Vegan Society.

———. 1983. *What Else is Cooking?* Enfield, U.K.: Vegan Society.

Bentham, Jeremy. 1780 [1907]. *Introduction to the Principles of Morals and Legislation*. Oxford: Clarendon Press.

Berry, Rynn. 2004. *Hitler: Neither Vegetarian Nor Animal Lover*. New York: Pythagorean Publishers.

Best, Steven and Anthony J. Nocella II, eds. 2004. *Terrorists or Freedom Fighters?* New York: Lantern Books.

Bondurant, Joan V. 1988. *Conquest of Violence*. Berkeley: University of California Press.

Borman, William. 1988. *Gandhi and Non-Violence*. Albany: State University of New York Press.

Brophy, Brigid. 1967. 'The Rights of Animals'. In *Don't Never Forget: Collected Views and Reviews*. New York: Holt, Rinehart and Winston.

———. 1985. 'Unlived Life—A Manifesto against Factory Farming'. Quoted in Jon Wynne-Tyson. 1985. *The Extended Circle*. Fontwell: Centaur Press, 1985, pp. 28–30.

Bryant, Arthur. 1969. *The Lion and The Unicorn*. London: Collins.

Ceserani, Victor and Ronald Kinton. 1970. *Practical Cookery*. London: Edward Arnold.

Church, Jill Howard. 2001. 'Pacheco after PETA: Seeking a Humane America'. In Kim Stallwood. 2001. *Speaking Out for Animals*. New York: Lantern Books.

Davis, Karen. 2004. 'Open Rescues: Putting a Face on the Rescuers and on the Rescued'. In Steven Best and Anthony J. Nocella II. 2004. *Terrorists or Freedom Fighters?* New York: Lantern Books.

Donaldson, Sue and Will Kymlicka. 2011. *Zoopolis: A Political Theory of Animal Rights*. Oxford: Oxford University Press.

Donovan, Josephine and Carol J. Adams, eds. 2007. *The Feminist Care Tradition in Animal Ethics*. New York: Columbia University Press.

Elliot, Rose. 1973. *Not Just a Load of Old Lentils*. Liss, Hants: White Eagle Publishing Trust.

———. 1974. *Simply Delicious*. Liss, Hants: White Eagle Publishing Trust.

———. 1988. *The Complete Vegetarian Cuisine*. New York: Pantheon Books.

Engel Jr., Mylan and Kathie Jenni. 2010. *The Philosophy of Animal Rights: A Brief Introduction for Students and Teachers*. New York: Lantern Books.

Evans, Rob and Paul Lewis. 2013. *Undercover: The True Story of Britain's Secret Police*. London: Faber & Faber.

Fisher, Elizabeth. 1979. *Woman's Creation*. New York: McGraw-Hill.

Flynn, Clifton P. 2012. *Understanding Animal Abuse: A Sociological Analysis*. New York: Lantern Books.

Fox, Michael W. 1984. 'Empathy, Humaneness and Animal Welfare'. In *Advances in Animal Welfare Science 1984/85*. Washington, D.C.: Humane Society of the United States.

Francione, Gary and Robert Garner. 2010. *The Animal Rights Debate*. New York: Columbia University Press.

Fudge, Erica. 2002. *Animal*. London: Reaktion Books.

———. 2008. *Pets*. Stocksfield: Acumen.

Gandhi, M. K. 2007. *The Story of My Experiments with Truth: An Autobiography*. London: Penguin.

———. 1999. *The Collected Works of Mahatma Gandhi*. Vol 13 (12 March 1919–25 December 1920). New Delhi: Publications Division Government of India, p. 241. <http://www.gandhiserve.org/cwmg/VOL013.PDF> (accessed February 11, 2014).

Garner, Robert. 1993. *Animals, Politics and Morality*. Manchester, England: Manchester University Press.

———., ed. 1996. *Animal Rights: The Changing Debate*. Basingstoke: Macmillan.

———. 2004. *Animals, Politics and Morality*. 2nd ed. Manchester: Manchester University Press.

———. 2005a. *Animal Ethics*. London: Polity Press.

———. 2005b. *The Political Theory of Animal Rights*. Manchester, England: Manchester University Press.

Gold, Mark. 1998. *Animal Century*. Charlbury, Oxon: Jon Carpenter Publishing.

Goodwin, Jeff and James M. Jasper, eds. 2003. *The Social Movements Reader*. Oxford: Blackwell.

Guillermo. Kathy. 1993. *Monkey Business*. Washington, D.C.: National Press Books.

Hall, Rebecca. 1984. *Voiceless Victims*. Hounslow, England: Wildwood House.

Harrison, Ruth. 1964. *Animal Machines*. London: Vincent Stuart.

Hawthorne, Mark. 2013. *Bleating Hearts: The Hidden World of Animal Suffering*. Winchester, England: Changemakers Books.

Hollands, Clive. 1980. *Compassion Is the Bugler*. Edinburgh: Macdonald Publisher.

Hopley, Emma. 1998. *Campaigning Against Cruelty: The Hundred Year History of the British Union for the Abolition of Vivisection*. London: BUAV.

IAS. 2003. 'The Institute for Animals and Society Action Plan'. Baltimore, Md.: Institute for Animals and Society.

Jones, Ken. 2003. *The New Social Face of Buddhism*. Boston: Wisdom Publications.

Kemmerer, Lisa. 2012. *Animals and World Religions*. Oxford: Oxford University Press.

Kemmerer, Lisa and Anthony J. Nocella II, eds. 2011. *Call to Compassion: Religious Perspectives on Animal Advocacy*. New York: Lantern Books.

Kenney, Matthew. 2011. *Everyday Raw Express*. Layton, Ut.: Gibbs M. Smith.

Kheel, Marti. 2008. *Nature Ethics*. Lanham, Md.: Rowman and Littlefield.

Kistler, John M. 2002. *People Promoting and People Opposing Animal Rights In Their Own Words*. Westport, Conn.: Greenwood Press.

Knight, Andrew. 2011. *The Costs and Benefits of Animal Experiments*. Basingstoke, U.K.: Palgrave Macmillan.

Libby, Ronald T. 1998. *Eco-Wars*. New York: Columbia University Press.

Lind af Hageby, Louise and Leisa Schartau. 1913. *The Shambles of Science*. London: The Animal Defence and Anti-Vivisection Society (fifth edition).

Linzey, Andrew, ed. 2009. *The Link Between Animal Abuse and Human Violence*. Brighton, U.K.: Sussex Academic Press.

London Borough of Islington. 1983. *The Animals' Charter*.

Luke, Brian. 2007. *Brutal*. Urbana: University of Illinois Press.

Lymbery, Philip and Isabel Oakeshott. 2014. *Farmageddon: The True Cost of Cheap Meat*. London: Bloomsbury.

Markarian, Mike. 2002. 'Sport Hunting: The Mayhem in Our Woods'. In Kim Stallwood, ed. 2002. *A Primer on Animal Rights*. New York: Lantern Books.

Mason, Jim. 1980. 'Need for Self-education'. *Agenda: A Journal of Animal Liberation*, no. 4 (October 1980).

———. 1993. *An Unnatural Order*. New York: Simon and Schuster.

Mason, Jim and Peter Singer. 1980. *Animal Factories*. New York: Crown.

Merz-Perez, Linda and Kathleen M. Heide. 2004. *Animal Cruelty: Pathway to Violence against People*. Walnut Creek, Calif.: AltaMira Press.

Midgley, Mary. 1980. *Beast and Man*. London: Methuen.

Milligan, Tony. 2013. *Civil Disobedience*. London: Bloomsbury.

Moss, Arthur. 1961. *Valiant Crusade: The History of the R.S.P.C.A.* London: Cassell.

Noske, Barbara. 1989. *Humans and Other Animals*. London: Pluto Press.

O'Sullivan, Siobhan. 2011. *Animals, Equality and Democracy*. Basingstoke: Palgrave Macmillan.

Paterson, David and Richard D. Ryder, eds. 1979. *Animals' Rights—A Symposium*. Fontwell, Sussex: Centaur Press.

Potter, Will. 2011. *Green Is the New Red*. San Francisco: City Lights Books.

Primatt, Humphrey. 1776. *A Dissertation on the Duty of Mercy and Sin of Cruelty to Brute Animals*. Available at <http://books.google.com /books?id=blwPAAAAIAAJ> (accessed February 10, 2014).

Radford, Mike. 2001. *Animal Welfare Law in Britain*. Oxford: Oxford University Press.

Randour, Mary Lou. 2000. *Animal Grace*. Novato, Calif.: New World Library.

Regan, Tom. 1983. *The Case for Animal Rights*. Berkeley: University of California Press.

———. 1987. *The Struggle for Animal Rights*. Clarks Summit, Penn.: International Society for Animal Rights.

———. 2004. *Empty Cages*. Lanham, Md.: Rowman and Littlefield.

Salt, Henry S. 1886. *A Plea for Vegetarianism and Other Essays*. Manchester: Vegetarian Society.

———. 1892. *Animals' Rights Considered in Relation to Social Progress*. London: George Bell & Sons Ltd.

———. 1907. *Humane Review* 8 (1907–8).

Saunders, Marshall. 1893. *Beautiful Joe*. Philadelphia: C.H. Bones.

Schaffner, Joan. 2010. *An Introduction to Animals and the Law*. Basingstoke: Palgrave Macmillan.

Sewell, Anna. 1877. *Black Beauty*. London: Jarrold.

Shapiro, Ken. 1994. 'The Caring Sleuth: Portrait of an Animal Rights Activist'. In Josephine Donovan and Carol J. Adams, eds. 2007. *The Feminist Care Tradition in Animal Ethics*. New York: Columbia University Press.

Singer, Peter. 1975. *Animal Liberation*. 2nd ed. New York: New York Review. 1990.

———., ed. 1985. *In Defence of Animals*. Oxford: Blackwell.

Smith, Linell. 2001. 'An Advocate for All Creatures'. *Baltimore Sun*, July 29.

Stallwood, Kim. 1996. 'Utopian Visions and Pragmatic Politics'. In Robert Garner, ed. 1996. *Animal Rights: The Changing Debate.* Basingstoke: Macmillan.

——., ed. 2001. *Speaking Out for Animals.* New York: Lantern Books.

——., ed. 2002. *A Primer on Animal Rights.* New York: Lantern Books.

——. 2004. 'A Personal Overview of Direct Action in the United Kingdom and the United States'. In Steven Best and Anthony J. Nocella II, eds. 2004. *Terrorists or Freedom Fighters?* New York: Lantern Books.

Thomas, Keith. 1983. *Man and the Natural World.* London: Allen Lane.

Towns, Sharon and Daniel Towns, eds. 2001. *Voices from the Garden.* New York: Lantern Books.

Vidal, John. 1997. *McLibel.* London: Macmillan.

Watson, Paul. 1996. *Ocean Warrior.* Toronto: Key Porter.

Westacott, E. 1949. *A Century of Vivisection and Anti-Vivisection.* Rochford, Essex, England: C.W. Daniel Company.

Wicklund, Freeman. 1998. 'Direct Action: Progress, Peril or Both?' In *The Animals' Agenda.* Baltimore: Animal Rights Network (July–August). See also Steven Best and Anthony J. Nocella II , eds. 2004. *Terrorists or Freedom Fighters?* New York: Lantern Books.

Williams, Erin E. and Margo DeMello. 2007. *Why Animals Matter.* Amherst, N.Y.: Prometheus Books.

Wise, Steve. 2000. *Rattling the Cage.* New York: Basic Books.

Wynne-Tyson, Jon. 1985. *The Extended Circle.* Fontwell, Sussex: Centaur Press.

Acronyms

AA—Animal Activists
AART—Action Animal Rescue Team
ADA—American Dietetic Association
ALDF—Animal Legal Defense Fund
ALF—Animal Liberation Front
ALL—Animal Liberation League
ARN—Animal Rights Network
ASH—Action on Smoking and Health
ASI—Animals and Society Institute
AWI—Animal Welfare Institute
AWT—Animal Welfare Trust
BHF—British Heart Foundation
BUAV—British Union for the Abolition of Vivisection
BWC—Beauty Without Cruelty
CAF—Culture and Animals Foundation
CAFO—Concentrated Animal Feeding Operations
CAFT—Coalition Against the Fur Trade
CAPS—Captive Animals Protection Society
CAW—Coordinating Animal Welfare
CCA—Canton Community Association
CCCWA—Christian Consultative Council for the Welfare of
    Animals
CEASE—Citizens to End Animal Suffering and Exploitation
CIWF—Compassion In World Farming
COK—Compassion Over Killing
CRAE—Committee for the Reform of Animal Experimentation

FARM—Farm Animal Reform Movement

FAWCE—Farm Animal Welfare Coordinating Executive

GECCAP—General Election Co-Ordinating Committee for Animal Protection

HEC—Humane Education Council

HSA—Hunt Saboteurs Association

HSUS—The Humane Society of the United States

IAS—Institute for Animals and Society

IBR—Institute for Behavioral Research

IFAW—International Fund for Animal Welfare

ISAR—International Society for Animal Rights

LACS—League Against Cruel Sports

MLA—Mobilisation for Laboratory Animals

NAVS—National Anti-Vivisection Society

NCSU—North Carolina State University

NEAVS—New England Anti-Vivisection Society

NIH—National Institutes of Health

NJEWC—National Joint Equine Welfare Committee

PCRM—Physicians Committee for Responsible Medicine

PETA—People for the Ethical Treatment of Animals

PSYETA—Psychologists for the Ethical Treatment of Animals

RCS—Royal College of Surgeons of England

RSPCA—Royal Society for the Prevention of Cruelty to Animals

SAF—Society and Animals Forum

SAVS—Scottish Anti-Vivisection Society

SEALL—South East Animal Liberation League

SNIP—Society for Neutering Islington's Pussies

SPCA—Society for the Prevention of Cruelty to Animals

UPC—United Poultry Concerns

VRG—Vegetarian Resource Group

VSUK—Vegetarian Society of the U.K.

Index

INDEX

About the Author

KIM STALLWOOD is an independent scholar and author on animal rights. He has more than thirty-five years of personal commitment and professional experience in leadership positions with some of the world's foremost animal advocacy organisations in the United Kingdom and in the United States. This includes Compassion In World Farming, British Union for the Abolition of Vivisection, People for the Ethical Treatment of Animals, and *The Animals' Agenda* magazine. He co-founded the Animals and Society Institute in 2005 and is their European Director. He is also Executive Director of Minding Animals International. His client organisations include Compassion In World Farming, League Against Cruel Sports, and GREY2K USA. As a volunteer, he served on the boards of directors of the Vegan Society and the RSPCA, and he is also the founding president of the Canton Community Association in Baltimore, Maryland, where he lived for eighteen years, where the city's first dog park was formed. He became a vegetarian in 1974, after working in a chicken slaughterhouse. He has been a vegan since 1976. He holds dual citizenship in the United Kingdom and in the United States. His website is www.kimstallwood.com.

About the Publisher

LANTERN BOOKS was founded in 1999 on the principle of living with a greater depth and commitment to the preservation of the natural world. In addition to publishing books on animal advocacy, vegetarianism, religion, and environmentalism, Lantern is dedicated to printing books in the U.S. on recycled paper and saving resources in day-to-day operations. Lantern is honored to be a recipient of the highest standard in environmentally responsible publishing from the Green Press Initiative.

www.lanternbooks.com

CPSIA information can be obtained at www.ICGtesting.com
Printed in the USA
BVOW05s1429210714

359612BV00001B/1/P